I0489424

# The Hand-Shaped Drawing System

# Vol. 1

Ideas, Illustrated and written by:

## Yuridia Ramirez Olvera

**D**iscover all you can do with your hands and a

Little bit of creativity, learn how to draw using the shape of your hands, it's easy and fun! Just put your hand on top of a piece of paper, outline it with a pencil or pen, then add some details, this way you can draw: a dinosaur, a butterfly, and why not, a birthday cake too. In this book you'll find drawings and the instructions of how to make them. I invite you to enter this world of hands, hope you have fun, and of course, wish you learn how to draw using this unique technique.

# First Exercise: Hand

**Put your hand on top of a piece of paper and outline it, then draw the finger nails (you can add some accessories for your hand if you want to). Now the names of each one of the fingers, like on the example.**

**1**

**2**

**3**

middle finger

ring finger

index finger

pinky

thumb

# How To Make A Mask

(First of all, you'll need a thick paper for the mask, but first let's practice drawing it on the book). Outline your hand on the position you see above, next, you outline on the same position your other hand; if you're not able to write with both hands, then you'll ask for someone's help. Then you cut it out and décor it the way you want; you can color it, you can glue to it glitter, feathers, whatever that comes you to the mind. Finally, make it a pair of holes, one on each side, so you put it an elastic to wear it.

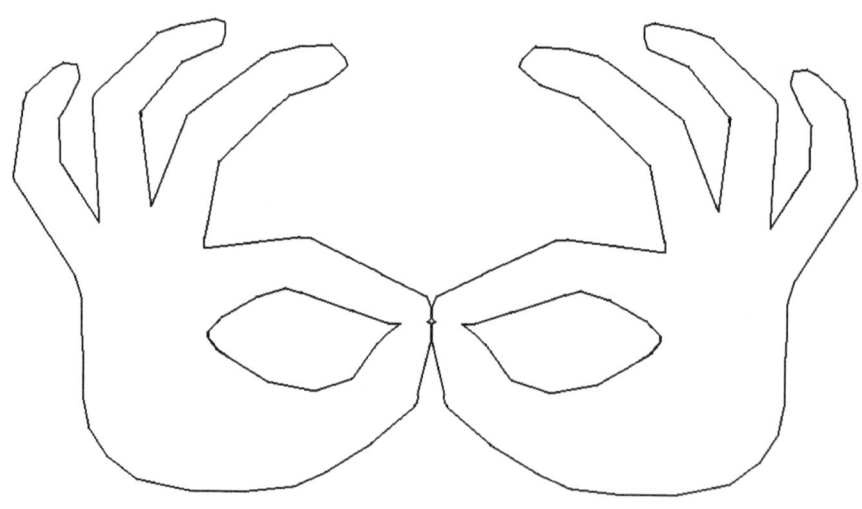

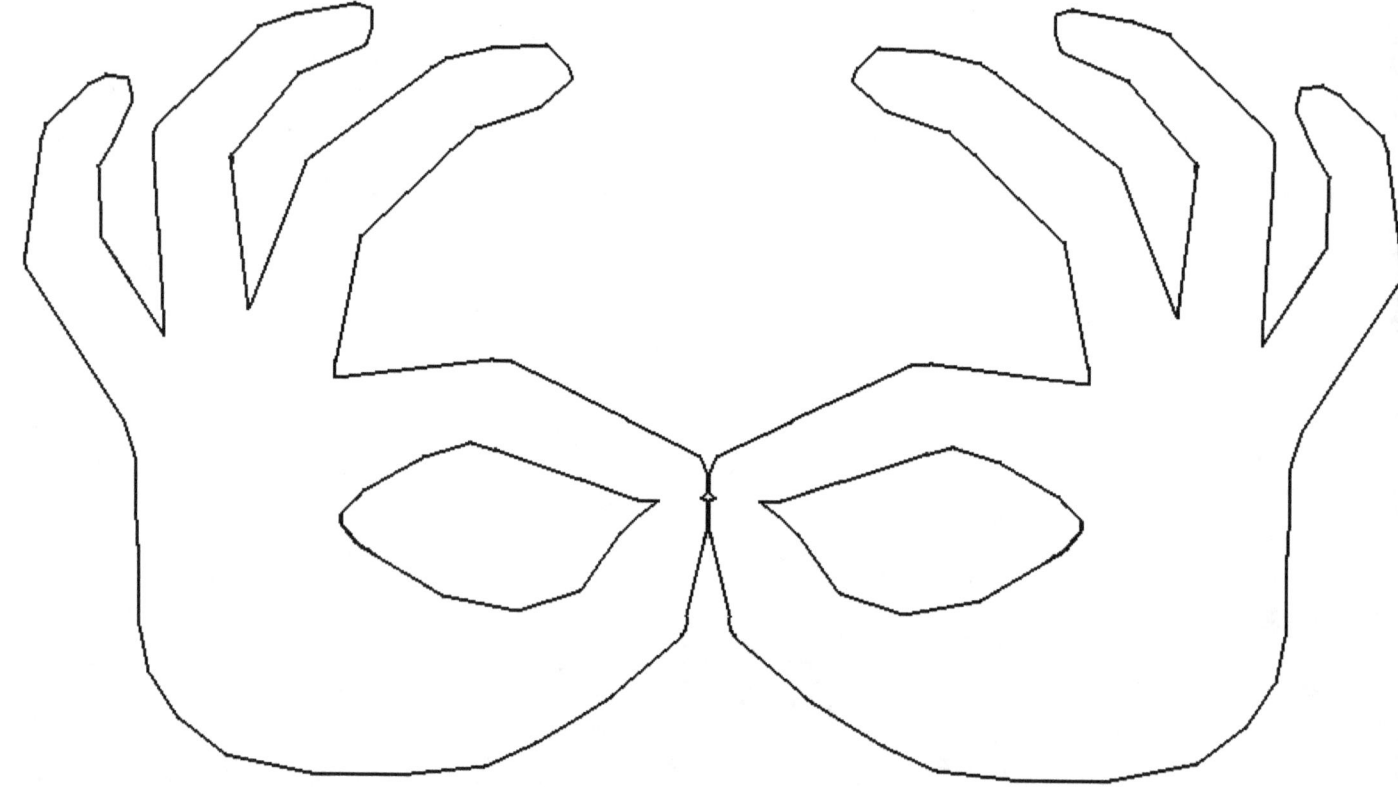

# Hen

**Put your hand on a piece of paper and outline it. The thumb will be the head; let's draw the beak, an eye and the cockscomb.**

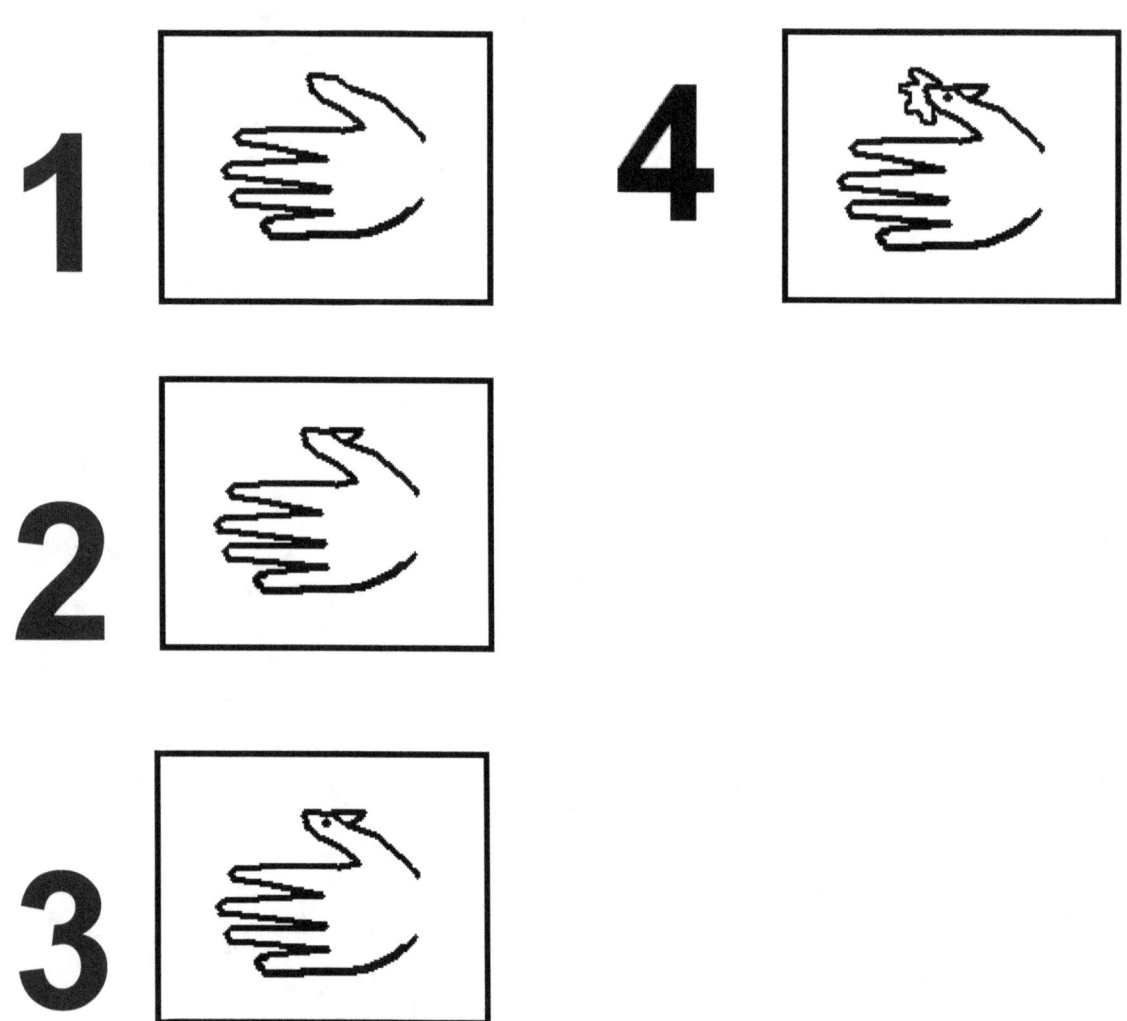

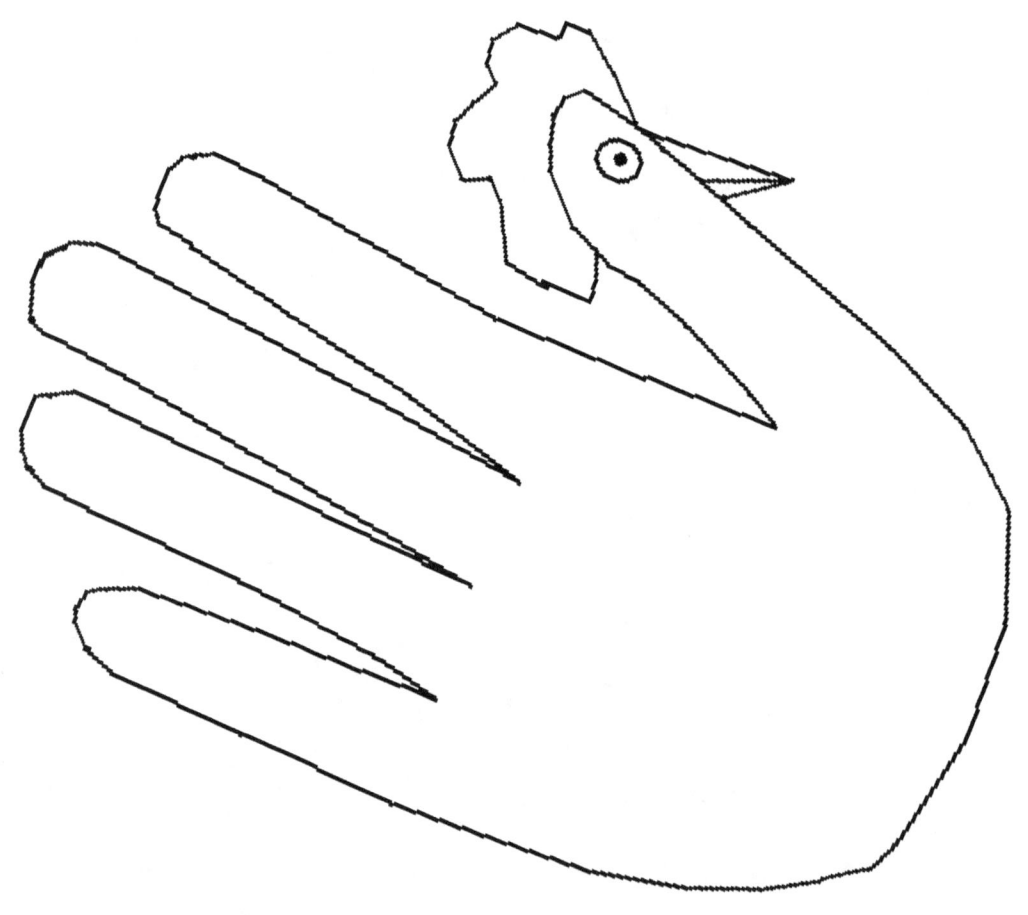

# Swans

Outline your hand on top of a paper, then you outline it again; but this time, with the hand's palm up, on a way that it looks like your both hands are one on the side of the other. Each hand will be a swan, then, you'll draw a beak and an eye to each one. Anything else? Water waves.

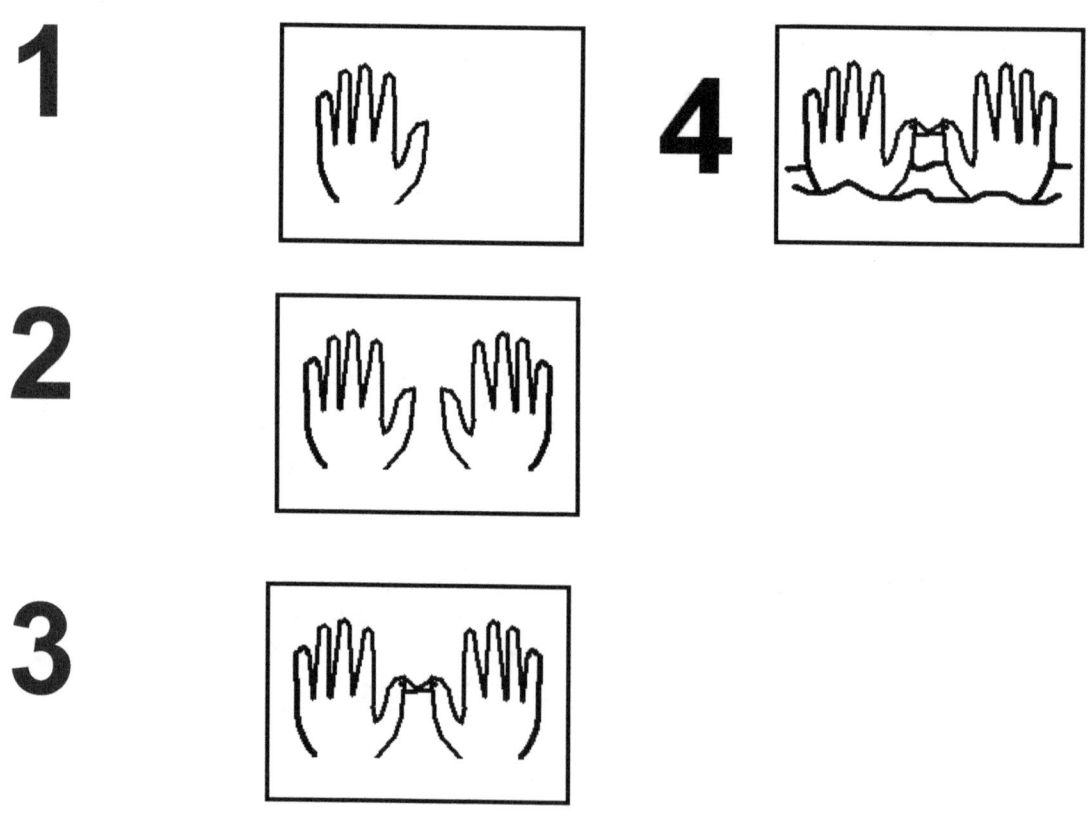

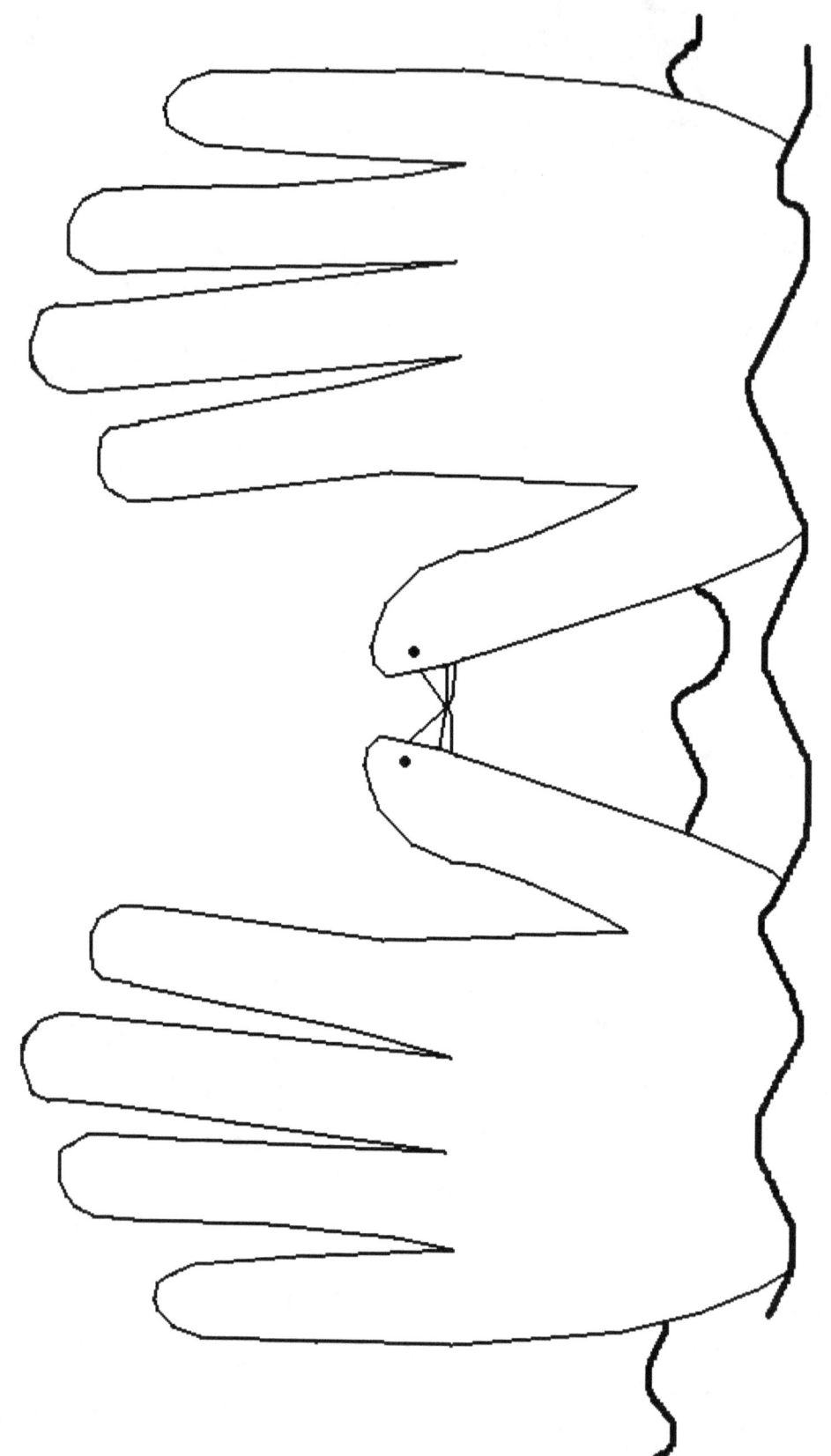

# Cactus

Outline your hand, draw oval son the tips of each one of the fingers. Draw a straight line on each finger, exactly in the middle, you'll also draw lines between the fingers. Now draw thorns all over the cactus and the desert sand.

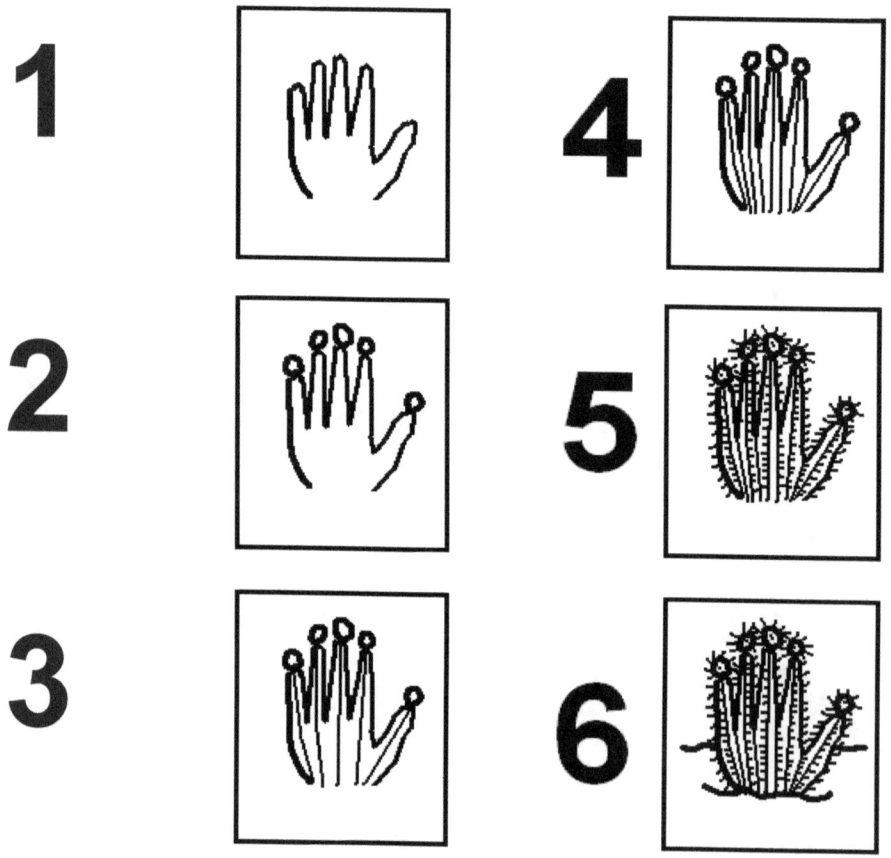

1

2

3

4

5

6

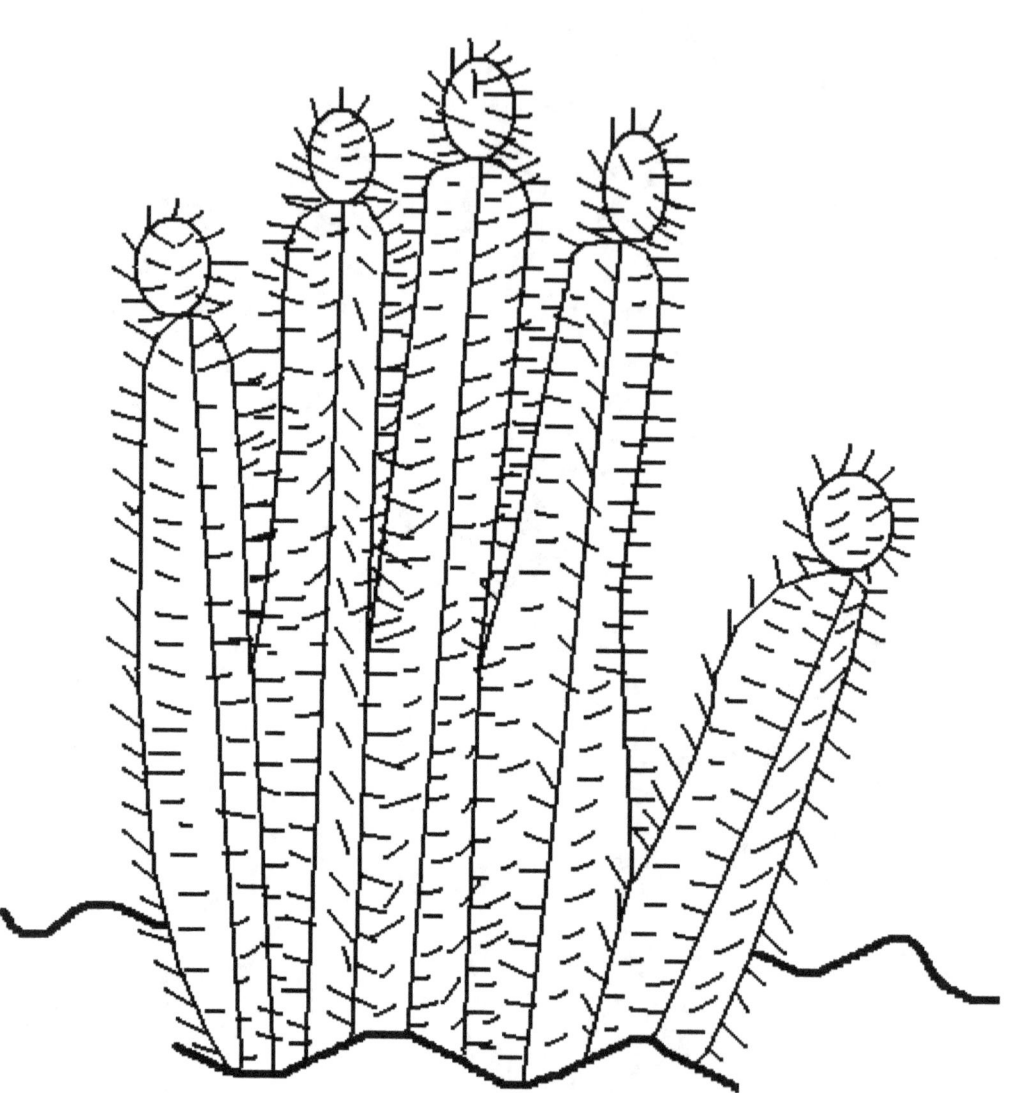

# Crown

Outline your hand without drawing the thumb, then you draw a Little bit curved line at the bottom. Let's draw circular gems, one on each finger, like if this ones were the nails, the same way you'll draw four more gems on the bottom. Finally, you can add zigzag lines from top to bottom.

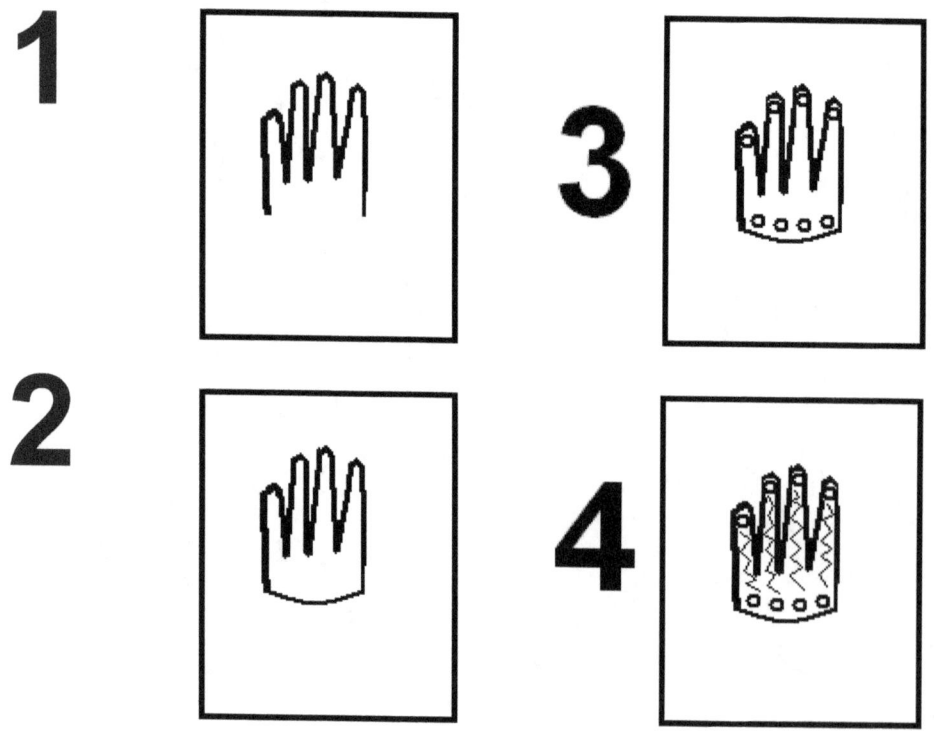

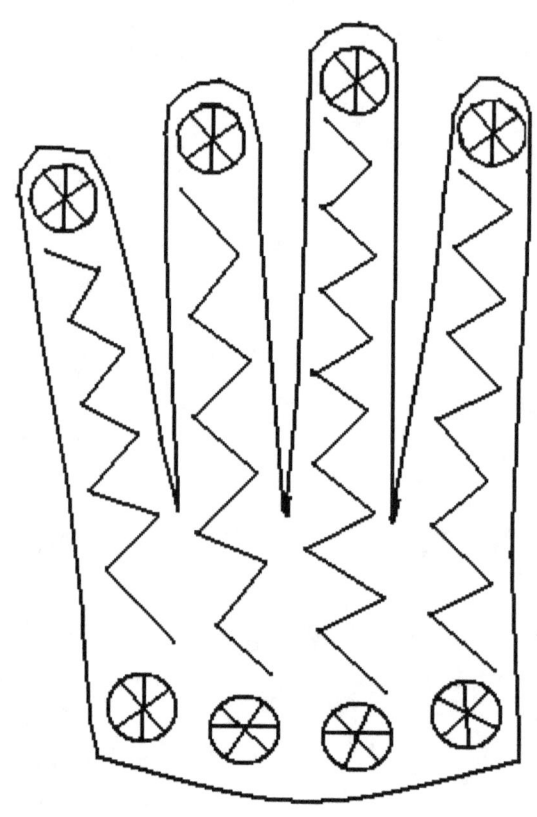

# Dinosaur Head

Separate the middle finger and ring finger forming a letter "v", outline your hand on this position. Then you draw the teeth, an eye, a nose's pore and finally the neck.

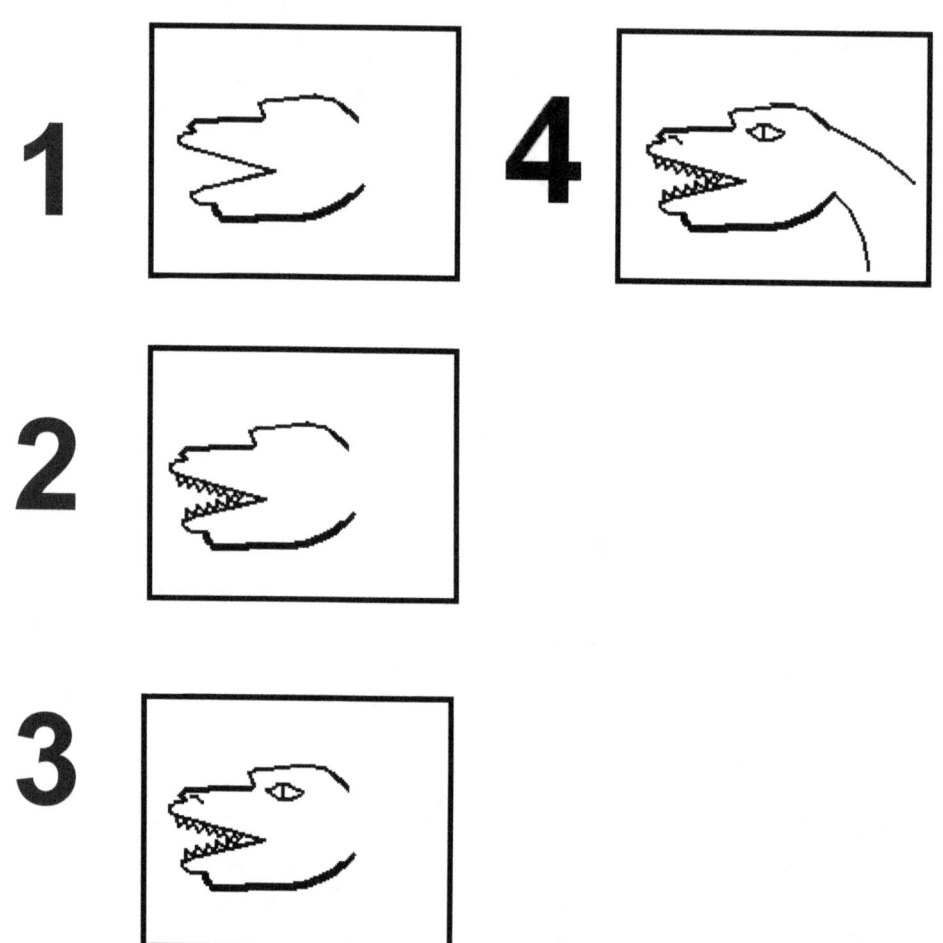

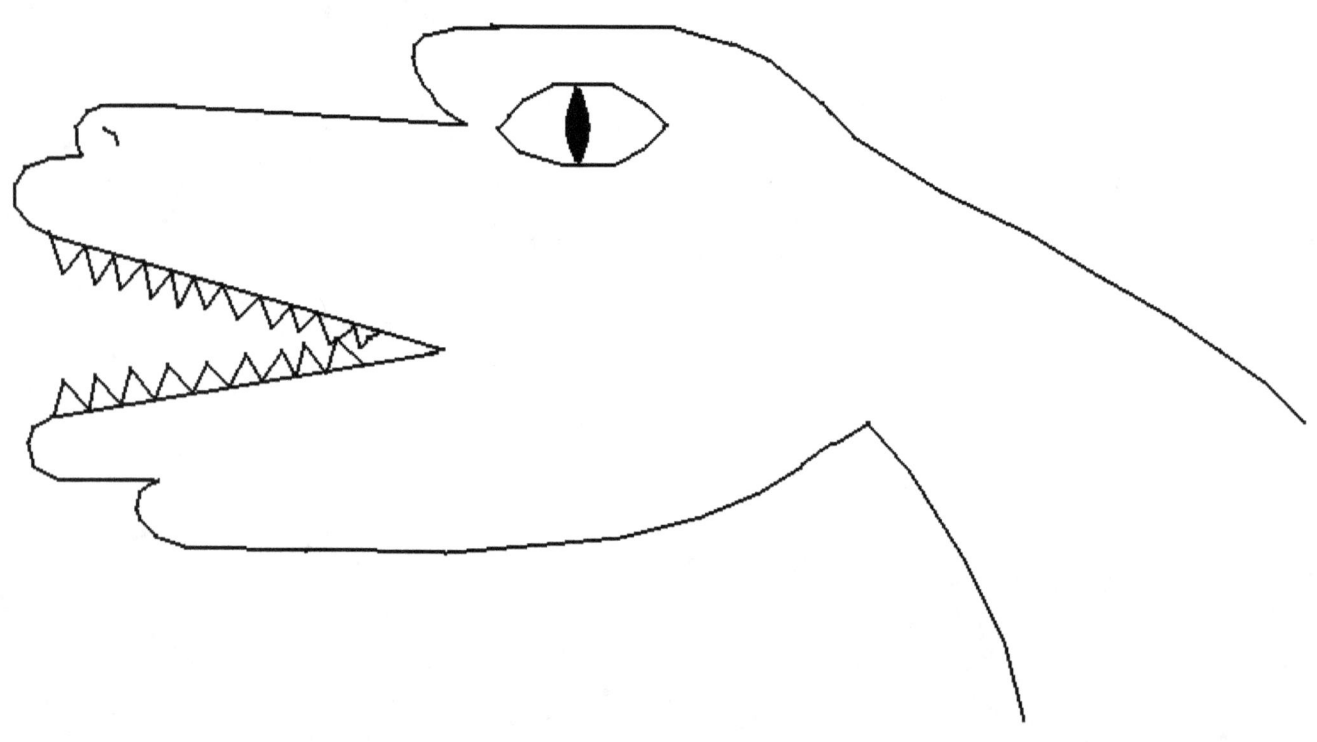

# <u>Dog</u>

Outline your hand on the same position as the dinosaur; making a letter "v" with the middle and ring fingers, only that this time, you'll also separate the thumb. Now draw the teeth, the nose, an eye, the inside part of the ear and the necklace, done.

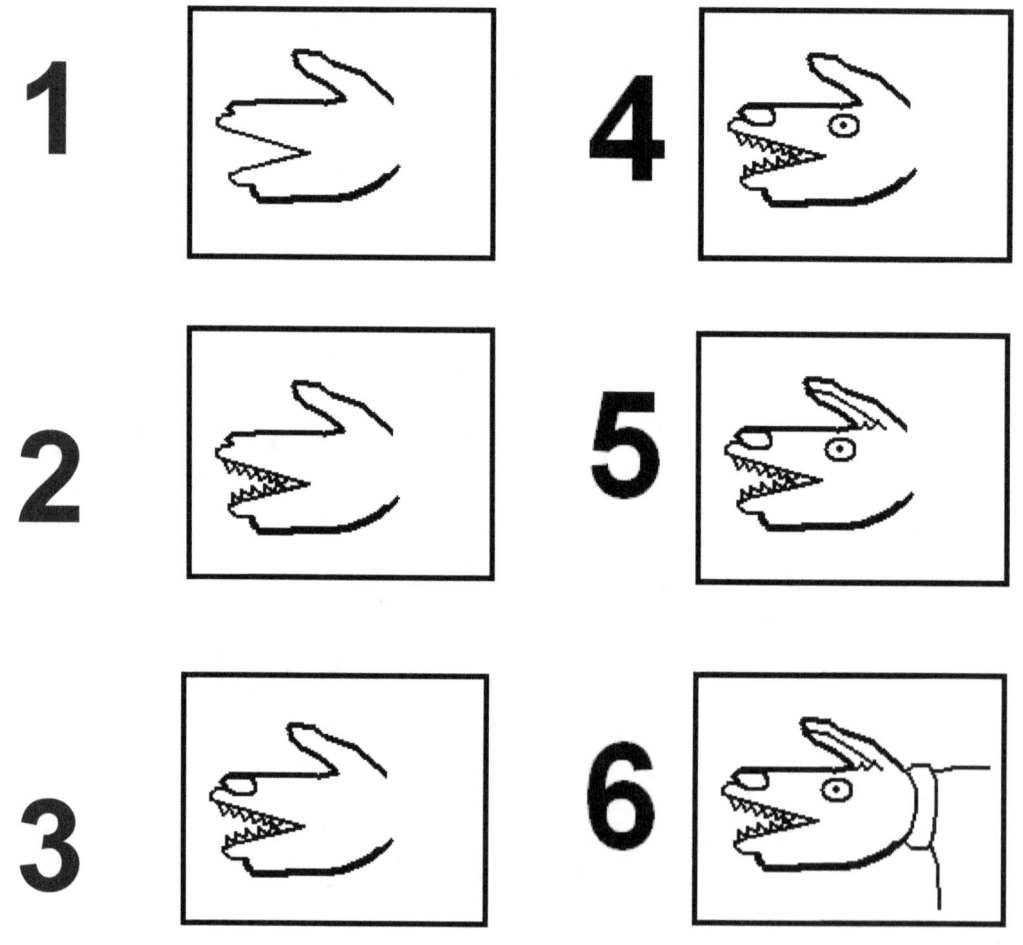

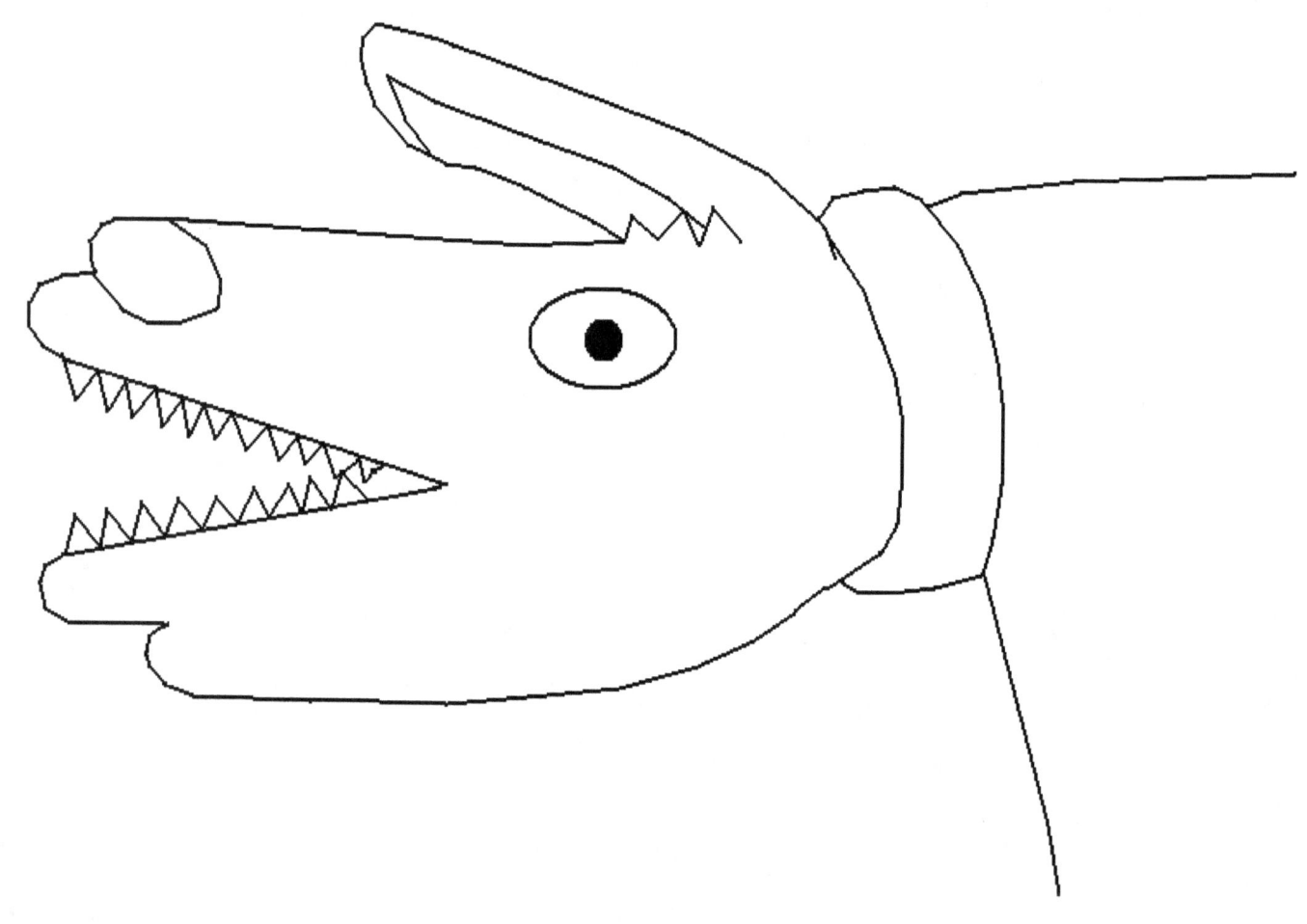

# Butterfly

Outline your open hand; with the thumb pointing down to the corner, and the middle finger pointing up to the corner. Outline your hand once more, on the same position, only that this time your palm will be down side up, as you see looks like your both hands are on the piece of paper. Your hands are the butterfly's wings, draw the body, the head, the eyes and antennas.

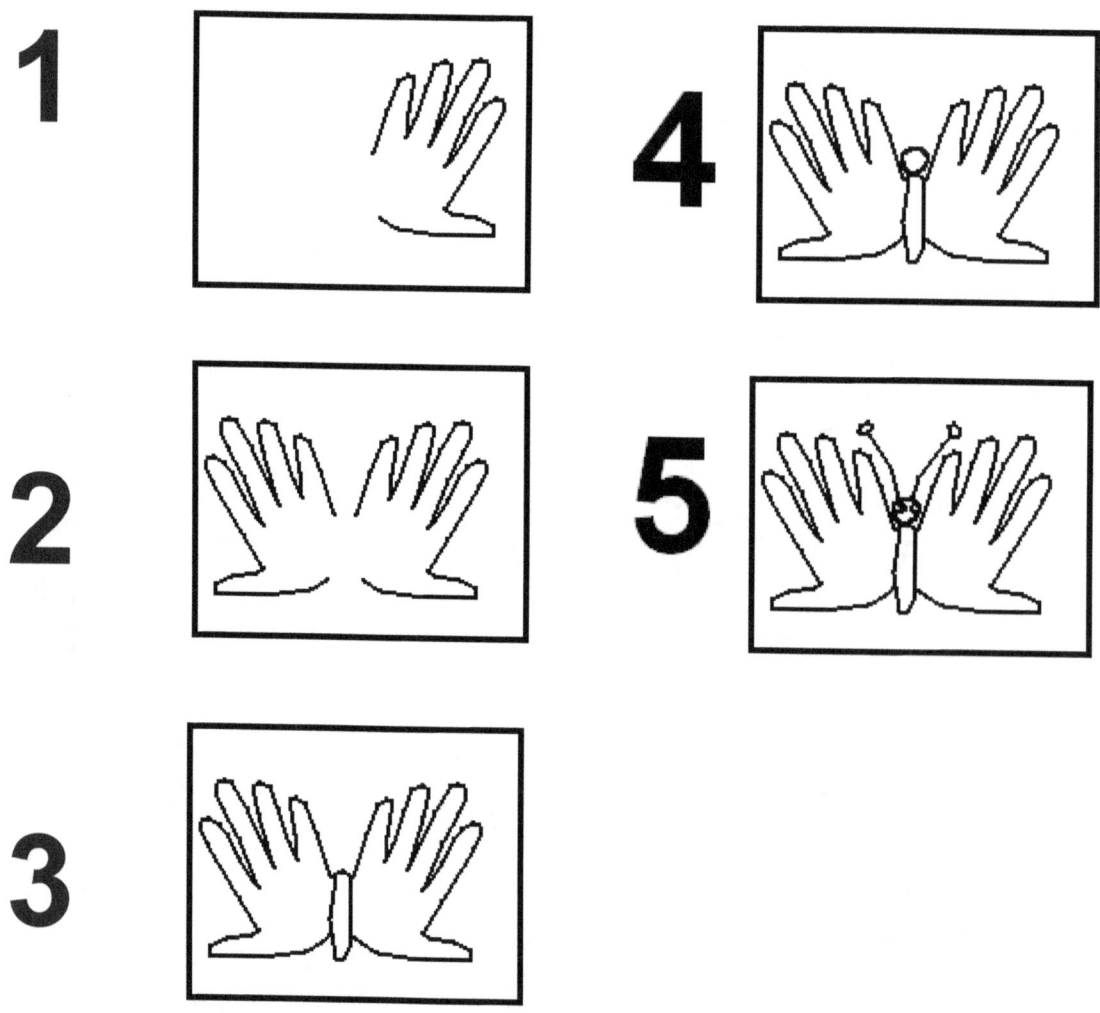

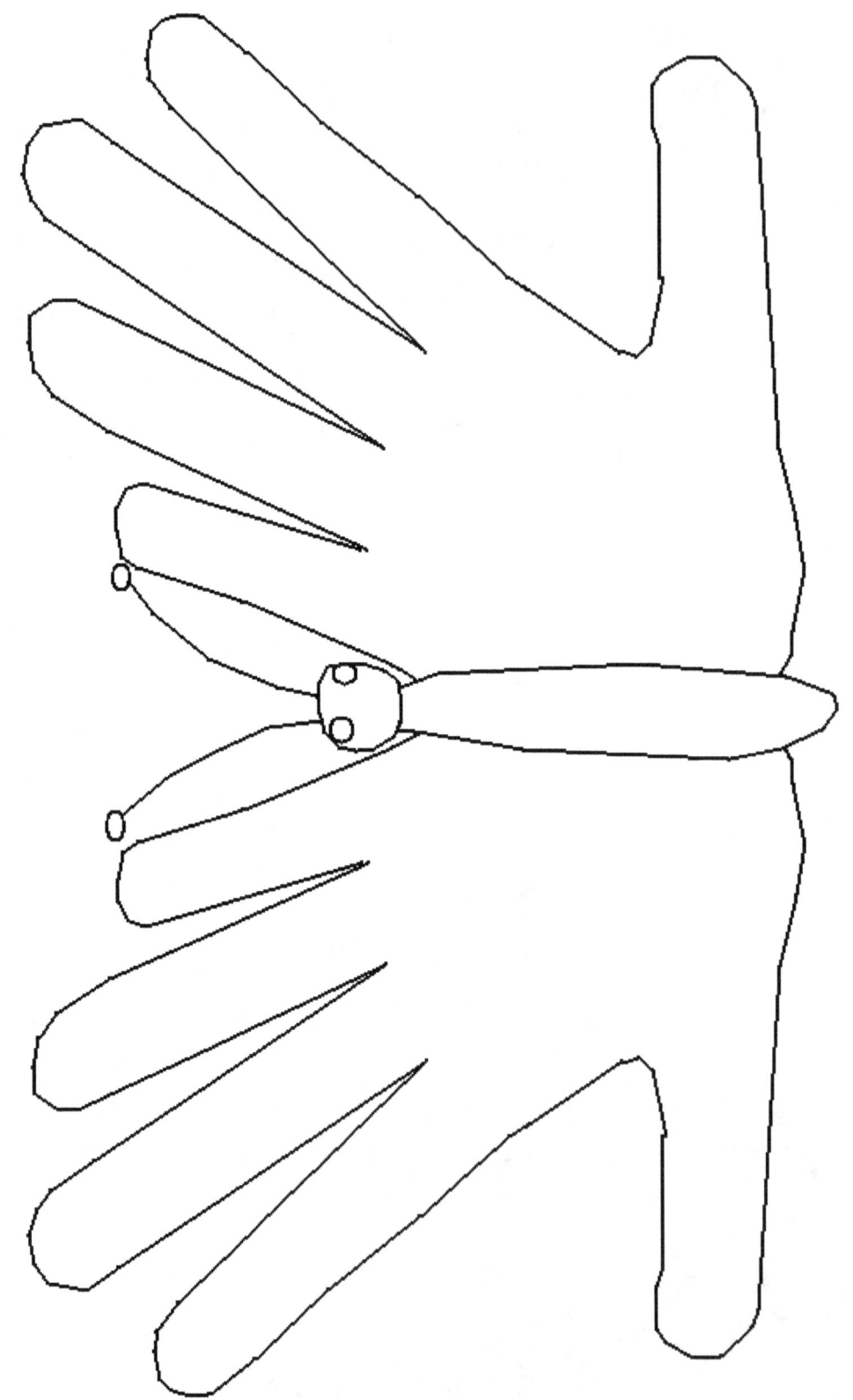

# Guy With Big Nose

Open your hand big and stretch your thumb the most you can, outline it like this. Draw an eye, an ear, the thumb is the nose; draw the mouth and neck below.

**1**

**2**

**3**

**4**

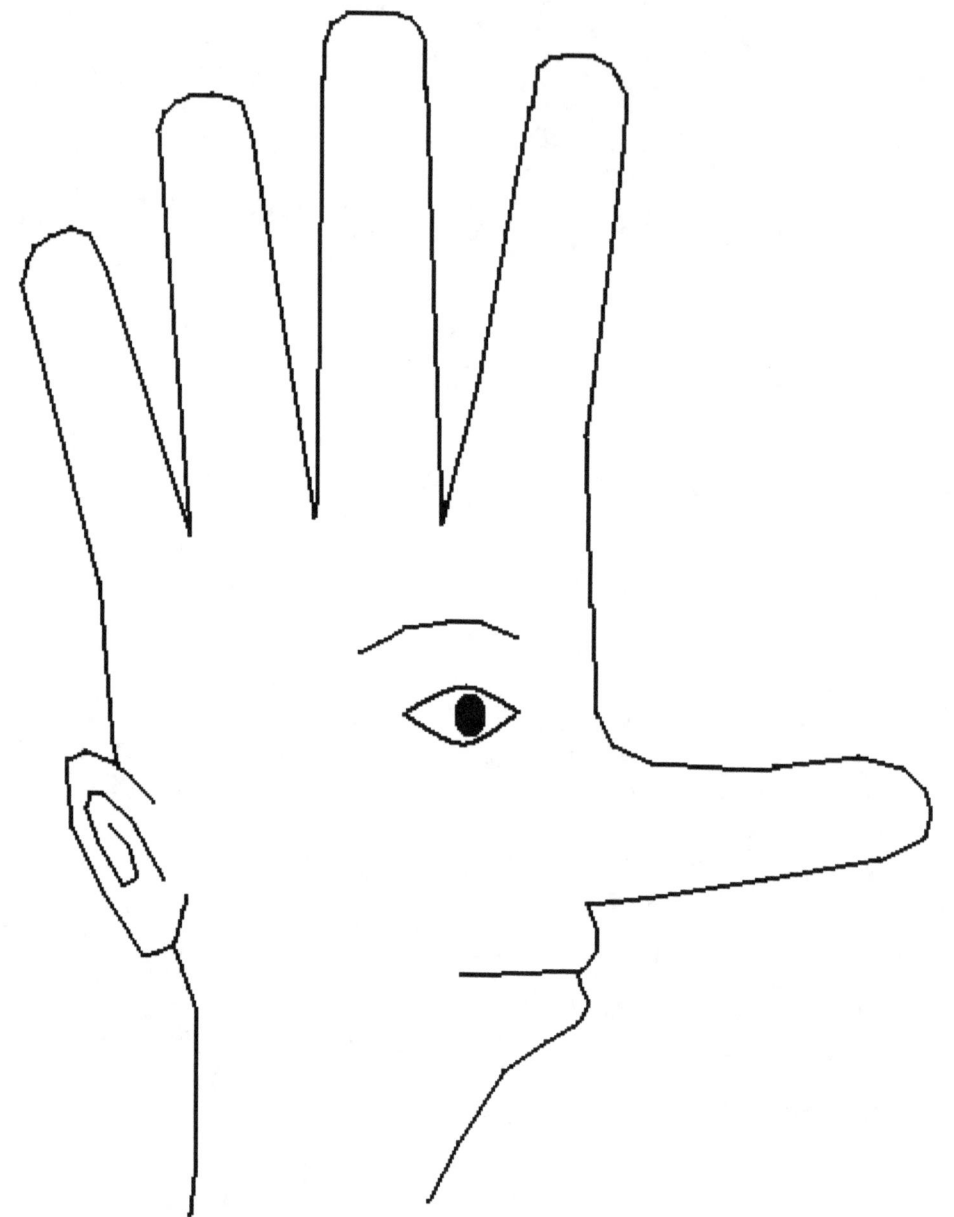

# Octopus

Open your hand, outline it, and turn the paper upside down; with fingers pointing down. Your fingers will be the tentacles of the octopus, draw the head, eyes and mouth. To finish, draw circles on the tentacles.

**1**

**2**

**3**

**4**

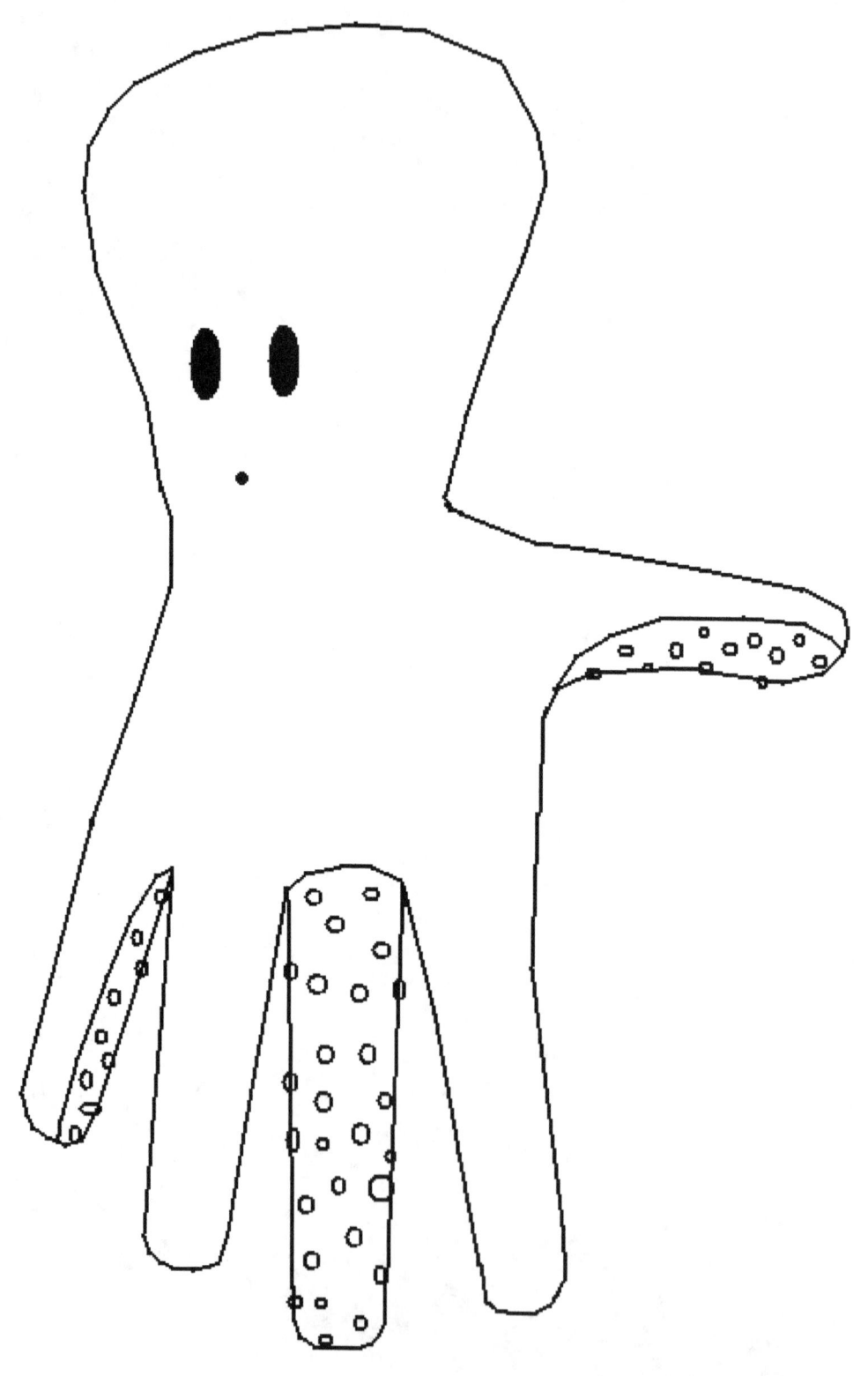

# House With Garden

Outline your hand as you see on the example, then, you outline it again on the same way, but this time with the hand's palm face up and by the side of the other. Now, draw the door, the windows, then, your thumbs are the grass and your other fingers are trees, so draw non-straight lines to divide the grass from the trees. As final touch, you can draw flowers or apples on the trees.

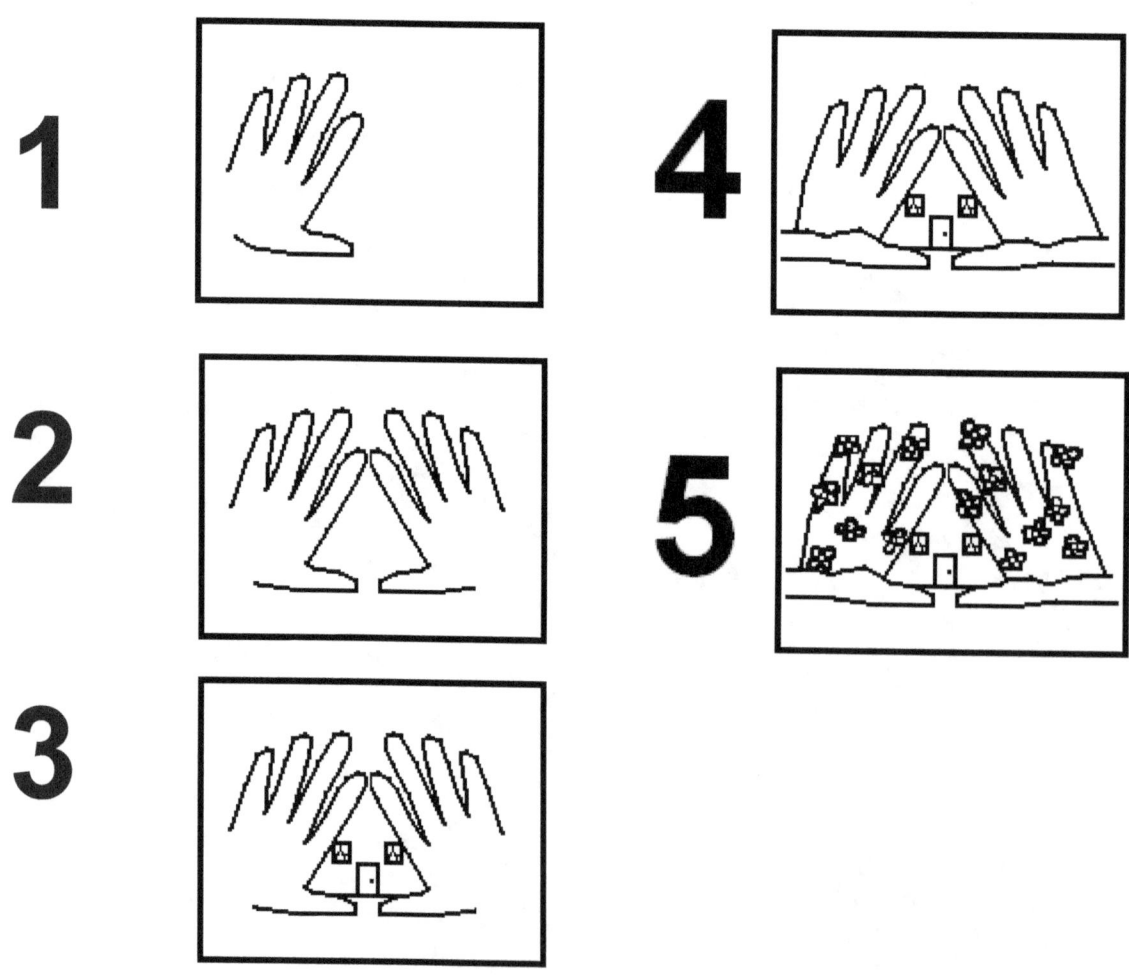

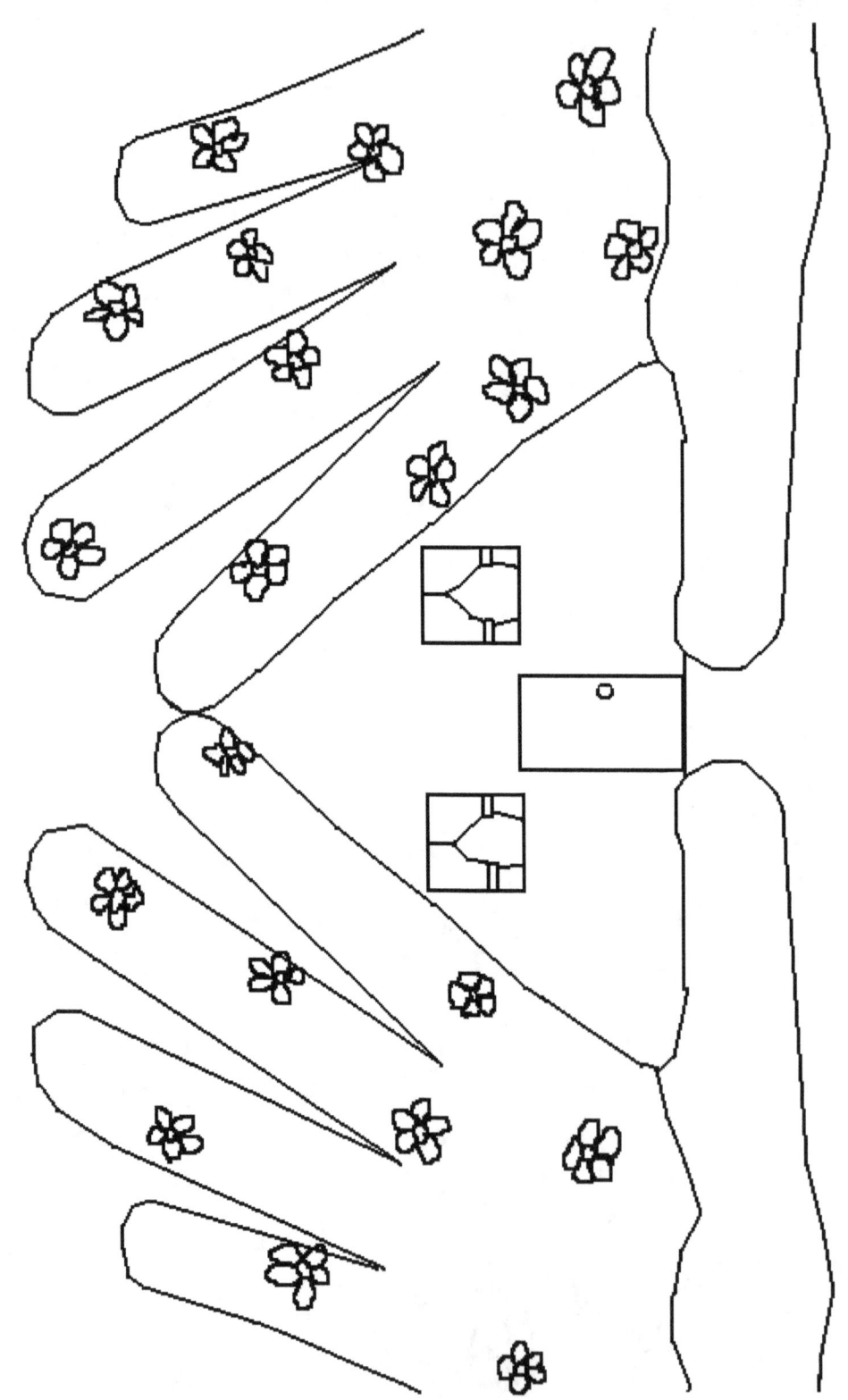

# Elephant

Open your hand and outline it at the center of the sheet of paper. Turn it upside down. Draw the elephant's ear, then a line going side to side of the hand without crossing over the ear. Draw a tail, an eye, a line going from the middle finger to the pinky (that'll be the elephant's belly) and a diagonal line on the other side if the middle finger (the breast). To finish, draw a circle on the tip of the thumb with two dots inside (the nose) and the tusk.

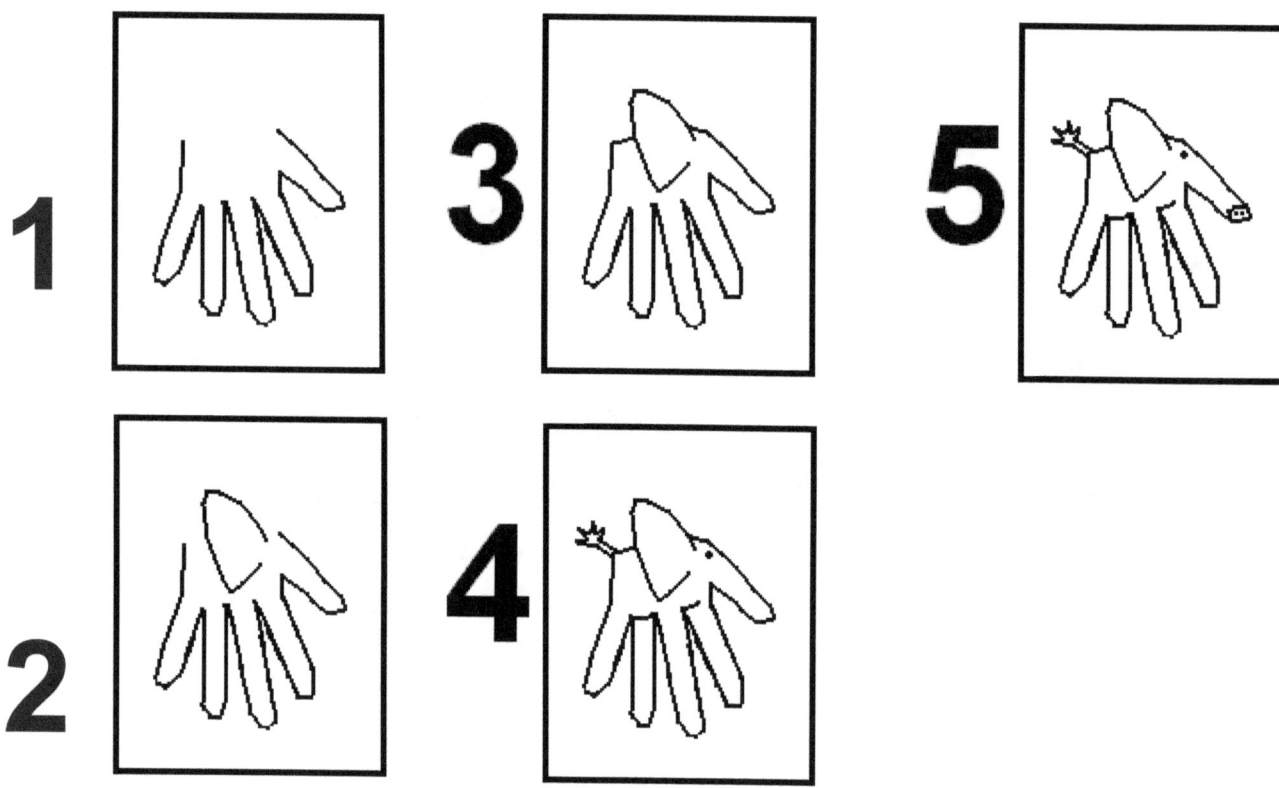

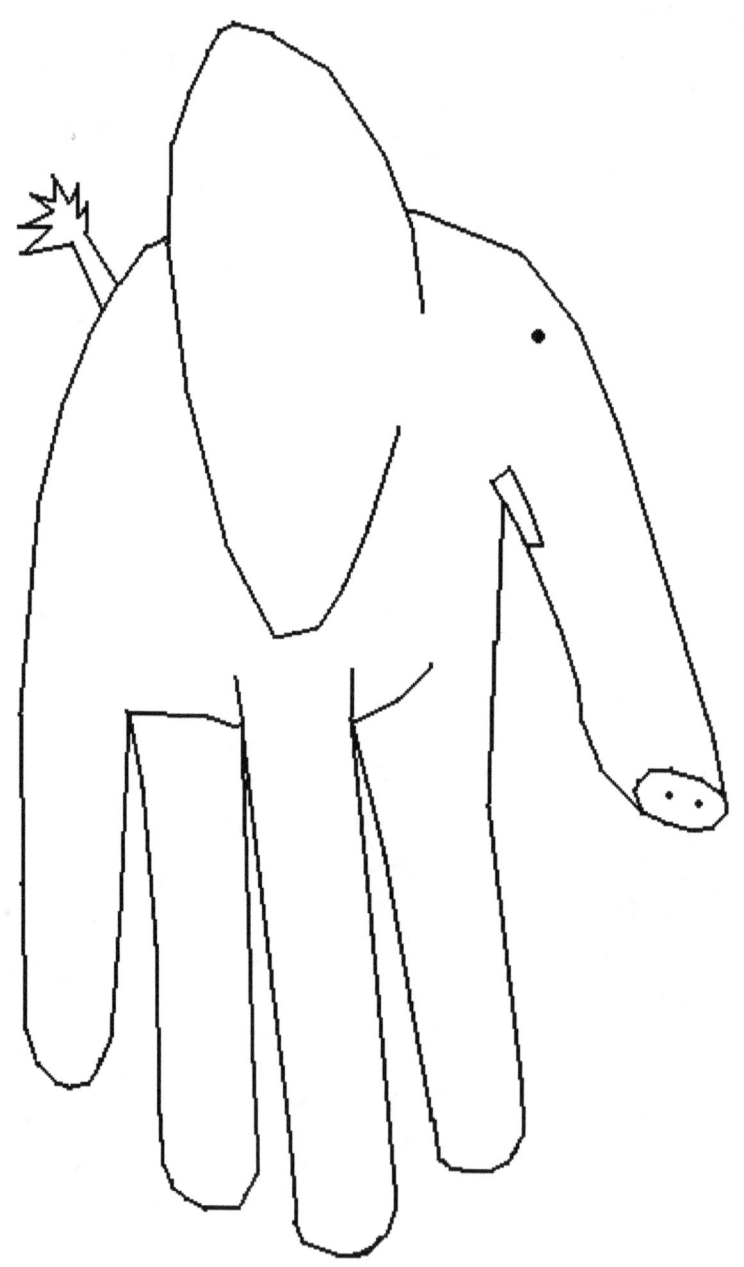

# Ice Cream Cone

Put your thumb forming a straight line with your arm and the other fingers forming a letter "v" with the thumb. You'll place your hand on the inferior part of the sheet of paper and outline it. Now you turn the paper upside down, draw a curved line on the top, and a stretched triangle at the bottom, that'll be the cone. Finally you draw squares on the cone.

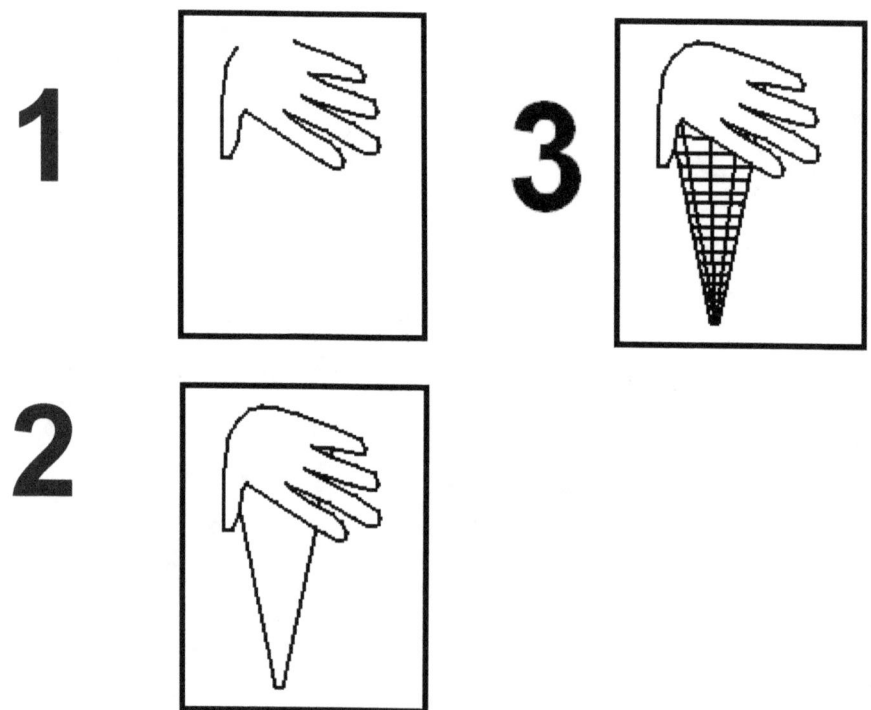

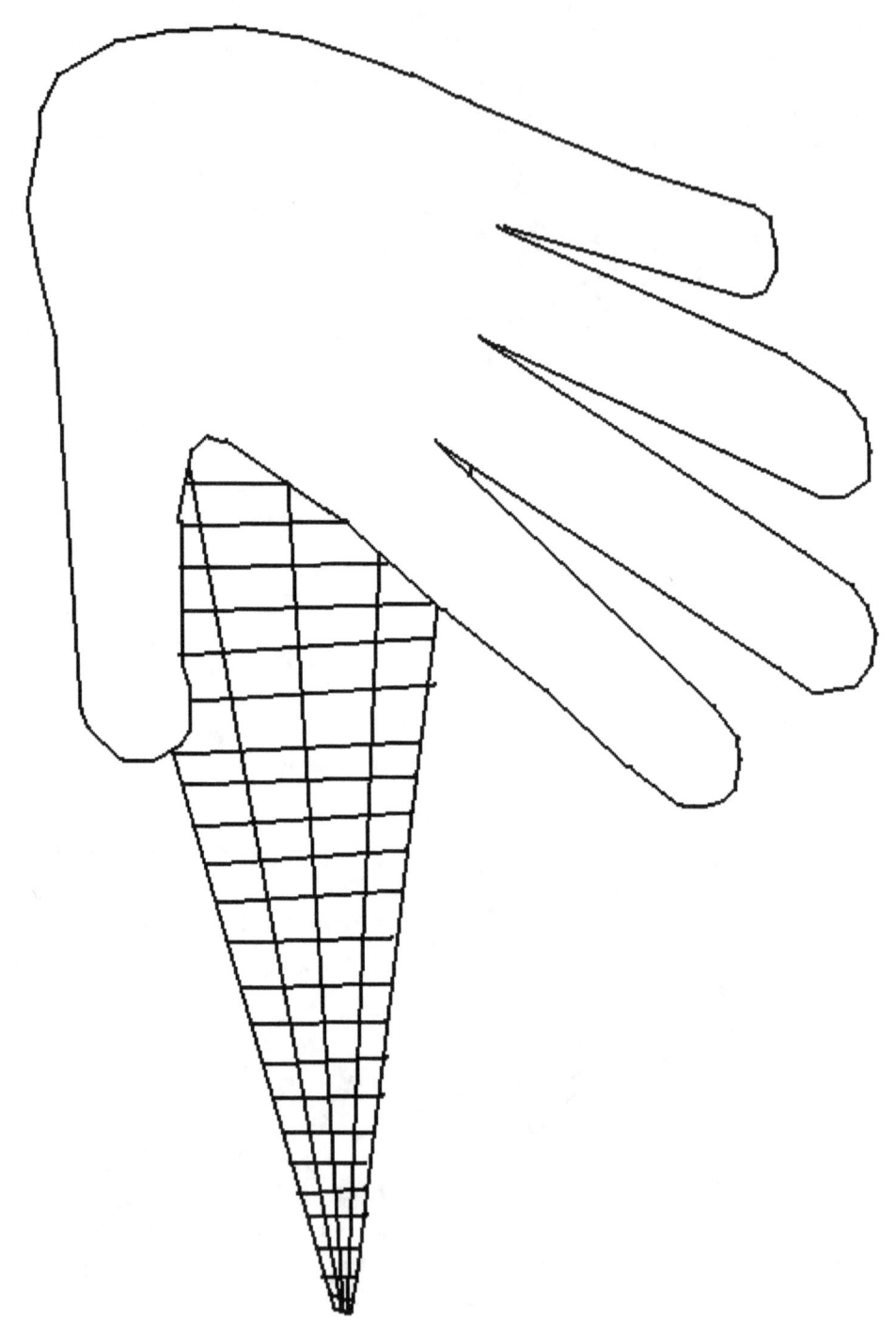

# <u>Tree</u>

Open your hand and outline it at the bottom of the paper, then you turn it upside down. Draw the tree's trunk and the grass. Finally, if you want to, you can draw flowers or fruits for your tree.

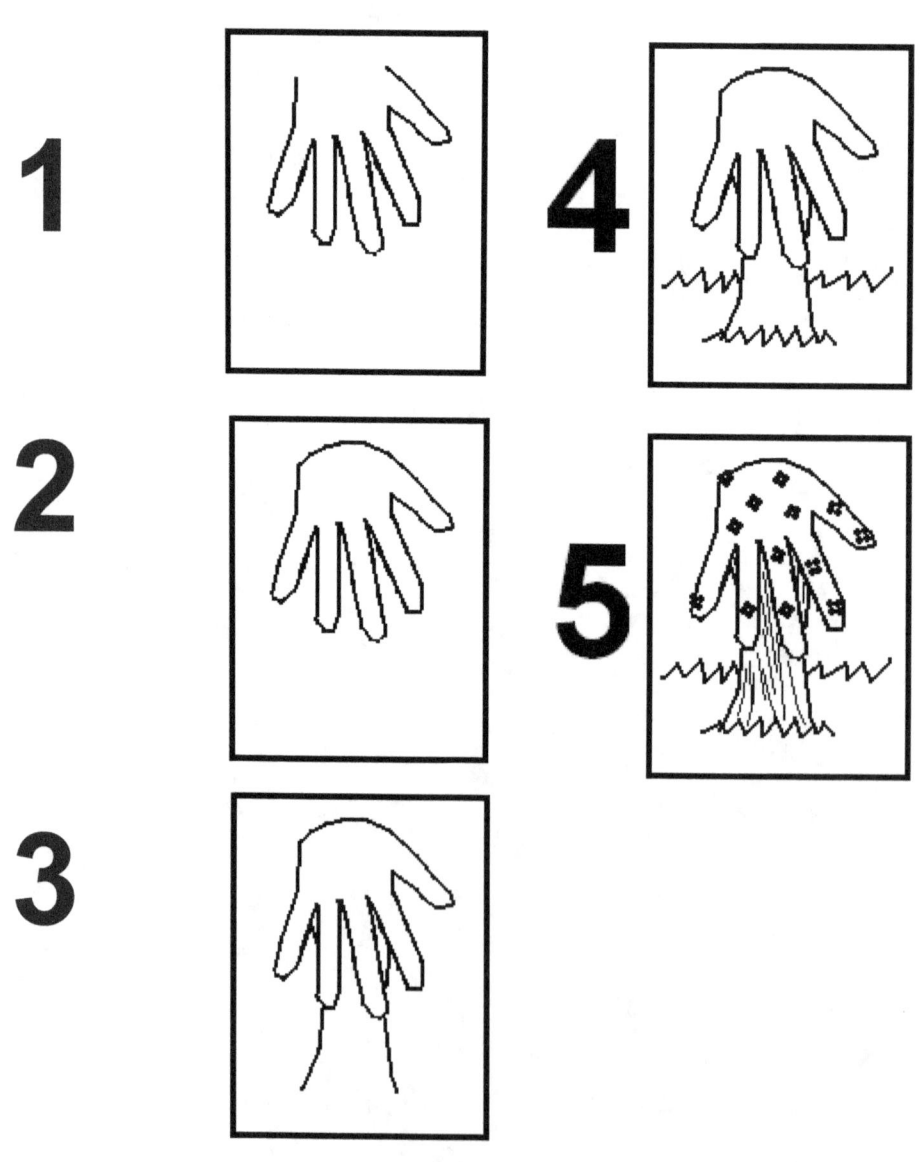

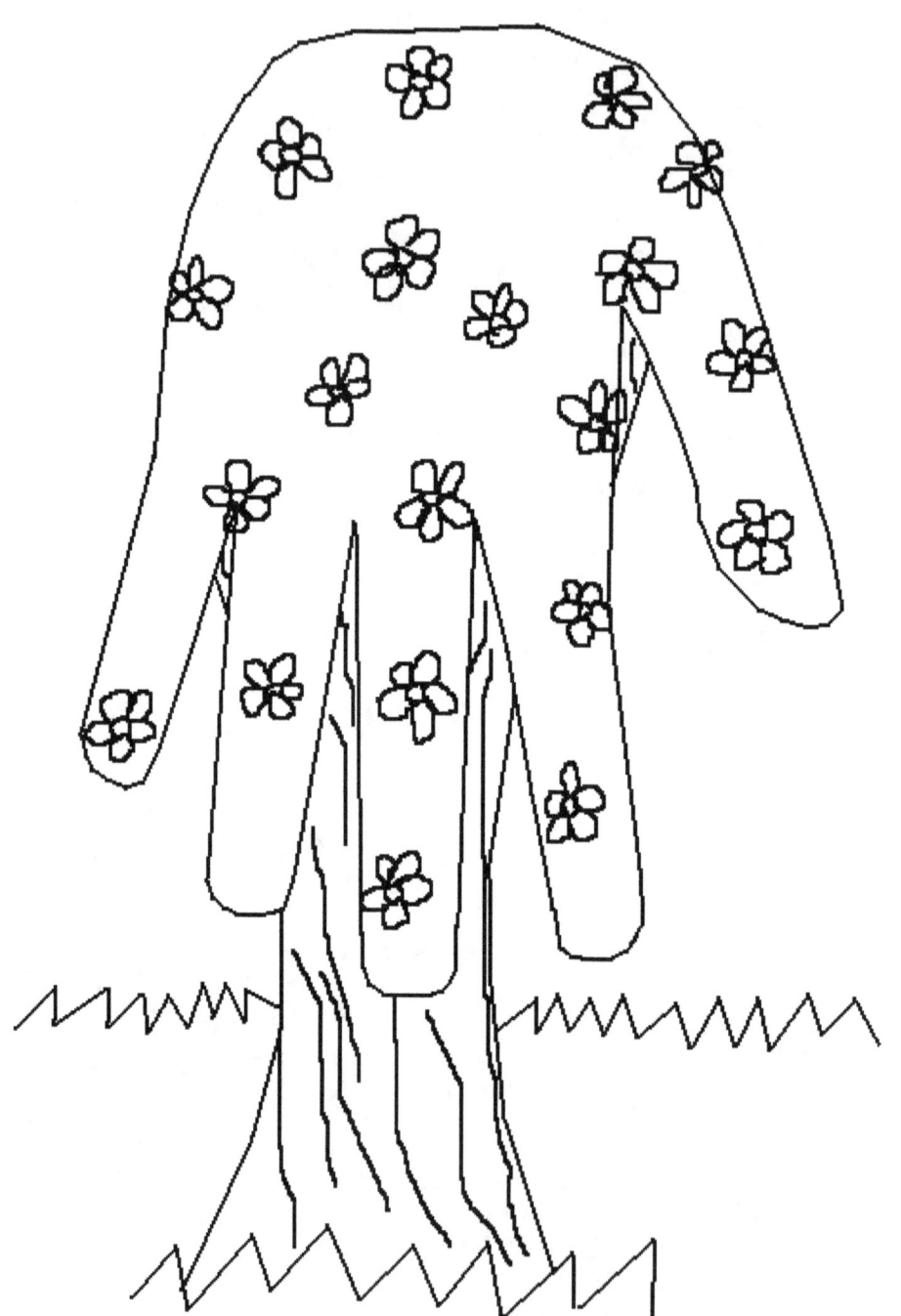

# Birthday Cake

Draw your open hand at the center of the sheet of paper. Turn it upside down. Draw the cake's candles and a curved line on the top from side to side of the hand. Now draw the cake's bread, if you have enough space, you can draw a plate.

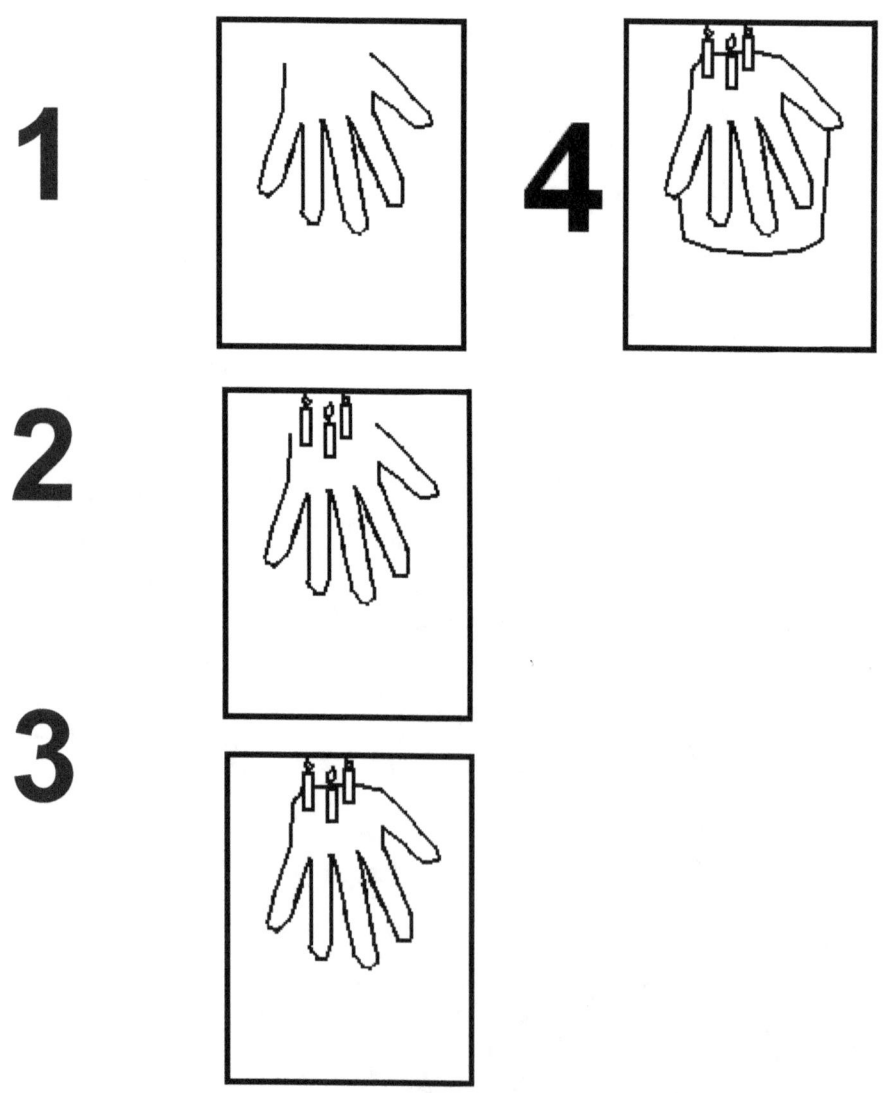

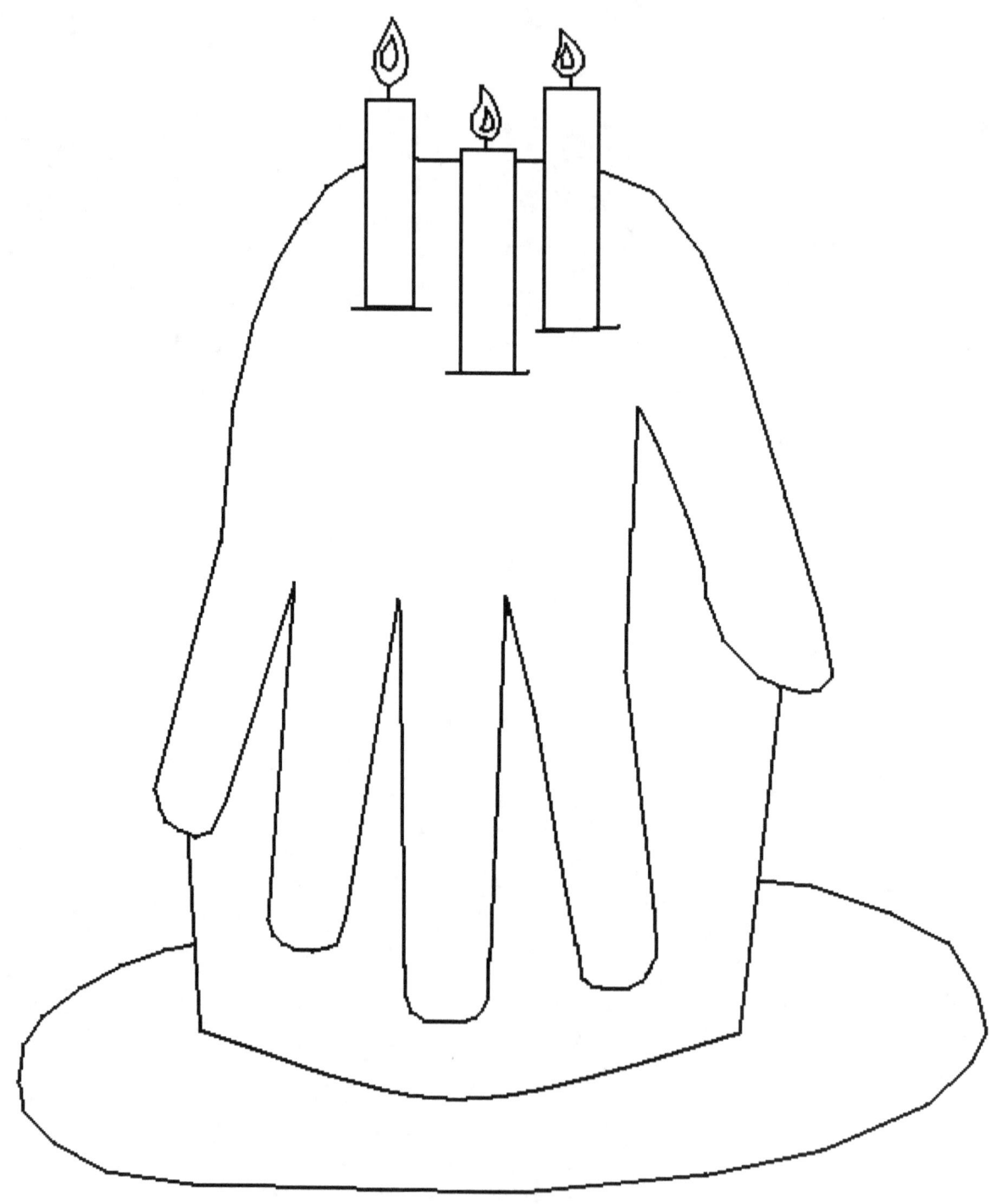

# Jar Of Tea

Put your hand on the position that looks like you're pointing to something with your thumb and outline it. Then, you draw the base of the jar, the handle, the top, and an orifice on the thumb.

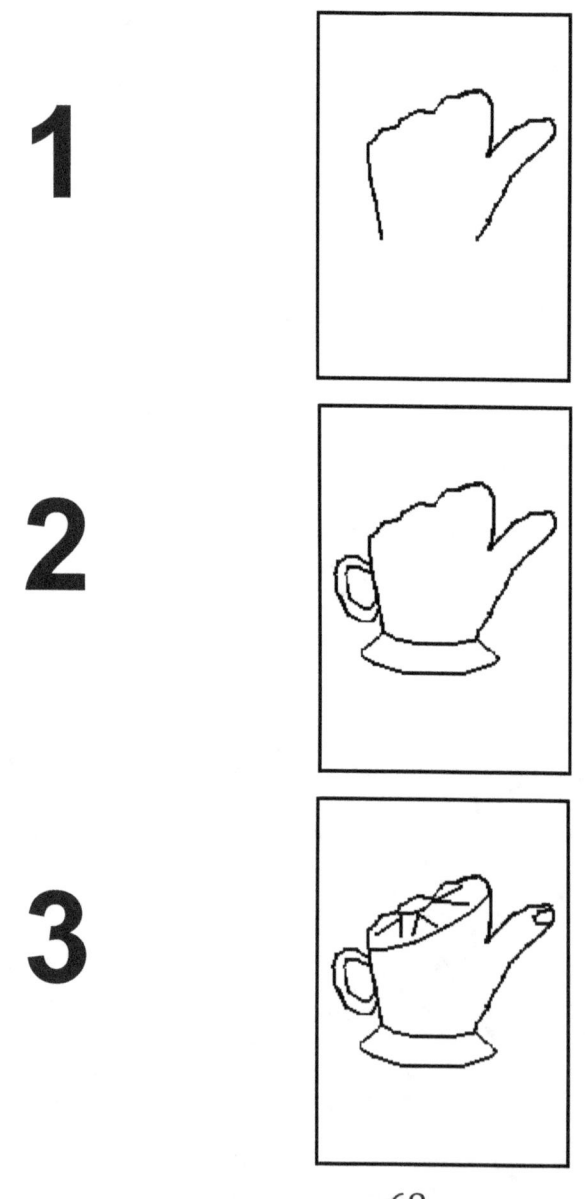

**1**

**2**

**3**

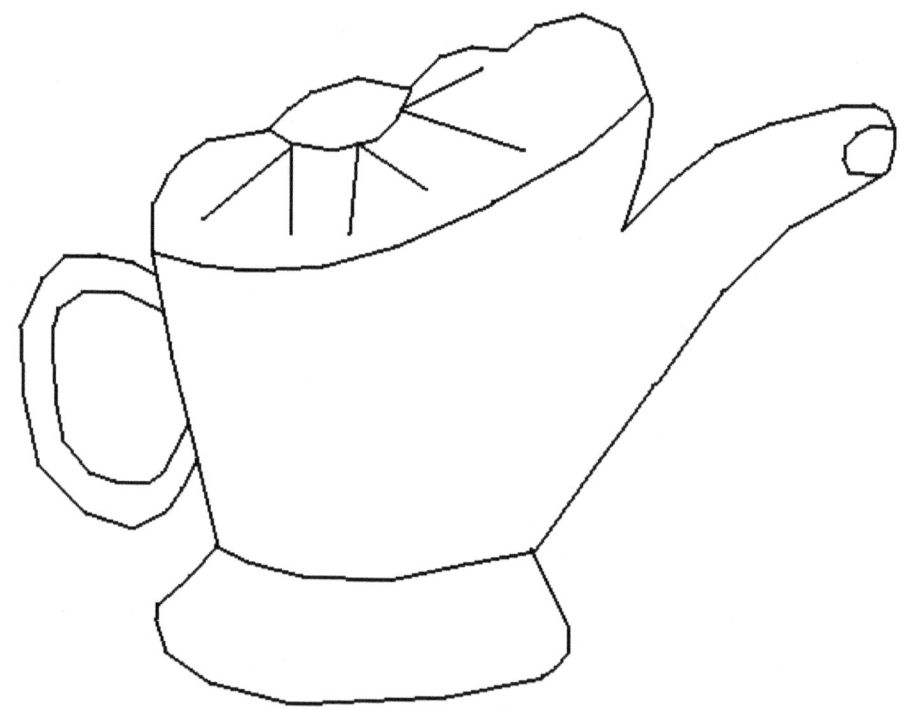

# Chicken

Put thumb and index finger together touching finger tips, the other fingers will be separated one from the other, outline your hand like this as you see on the illustrations. Draw the chicken's belly, beak, and an eye and feet.

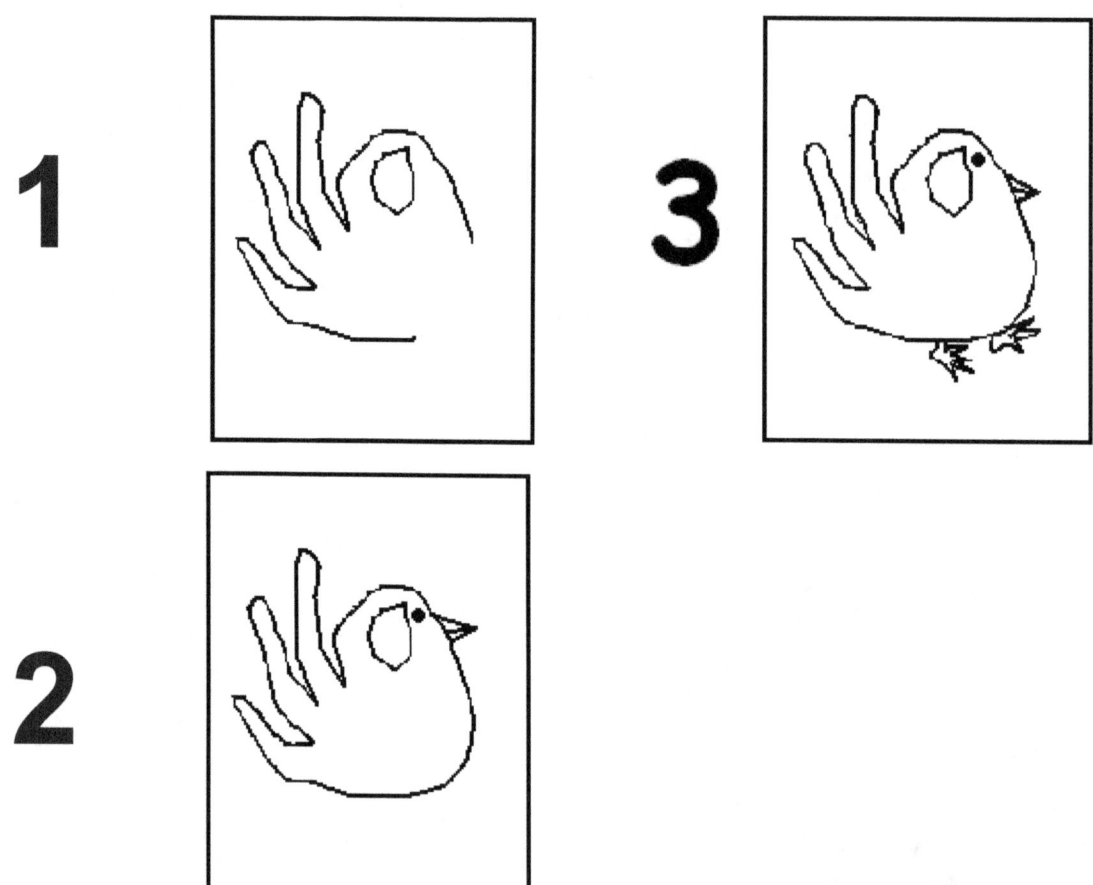

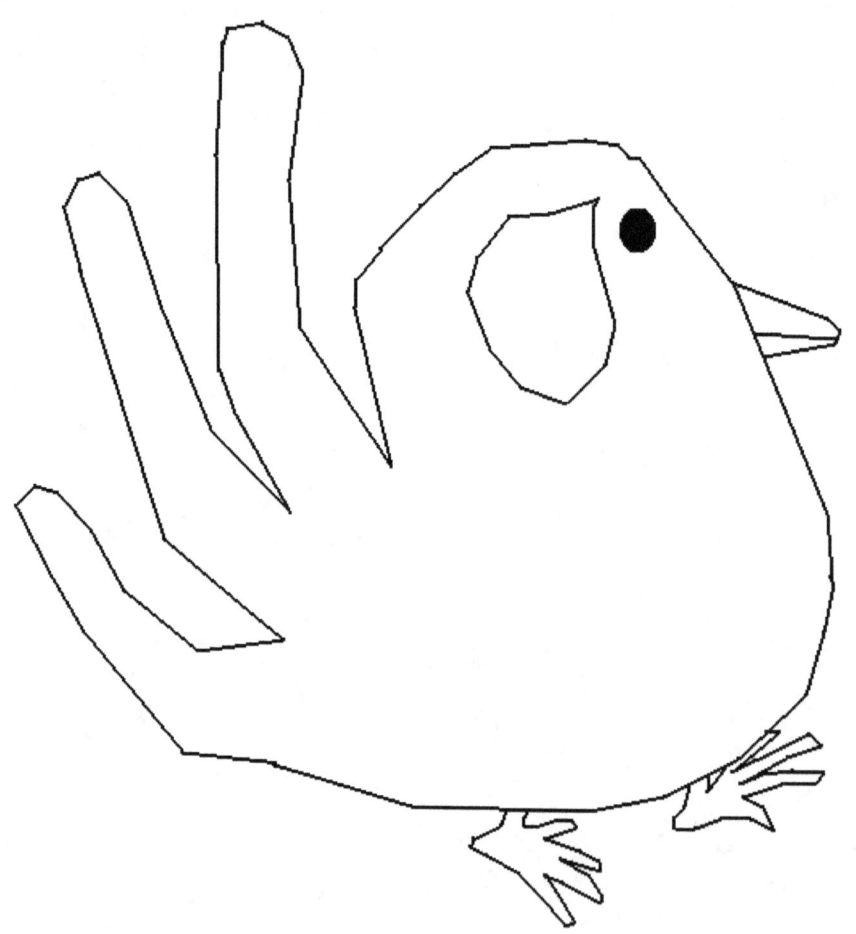

# Snake

Put your thumb pointing up, like this you'll draw your hand. The thumb will be the head of our snake, so let's draw an eye and the tongue. Then, on each one of your knuckles make a circle, so it looks like the snake is coiled up, and the last one (the pinky) will be the tail.

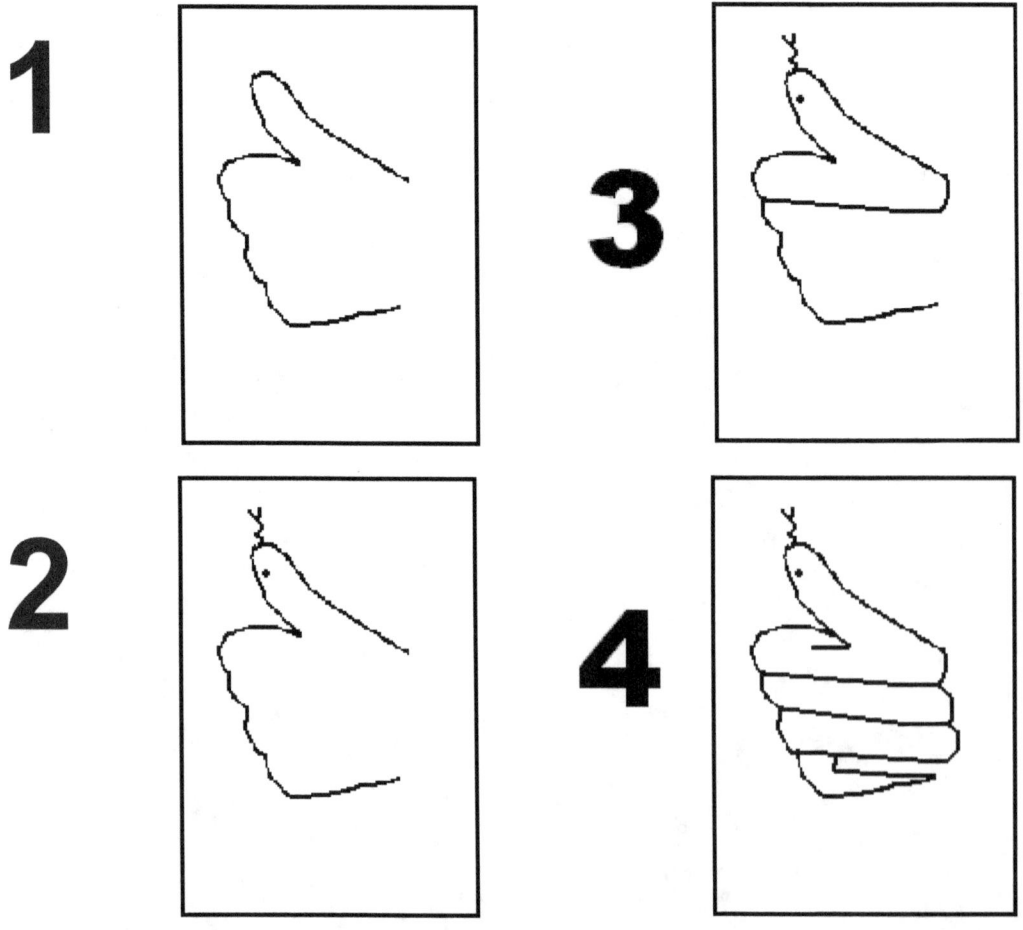

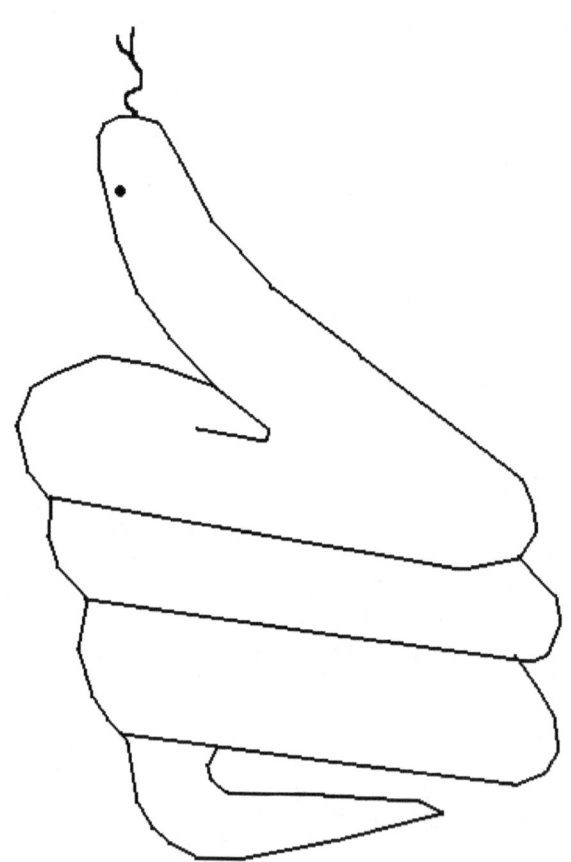

# A Girl

Place your hand at the bottom of the paper, with the thumb and the rest of the fingers making a letter "v", outline your hand. Turn the paper upside down. Your hand will be the girl's hair. Then, draw her face, eyes and mouth. Below the thumb, draw a pony tail.

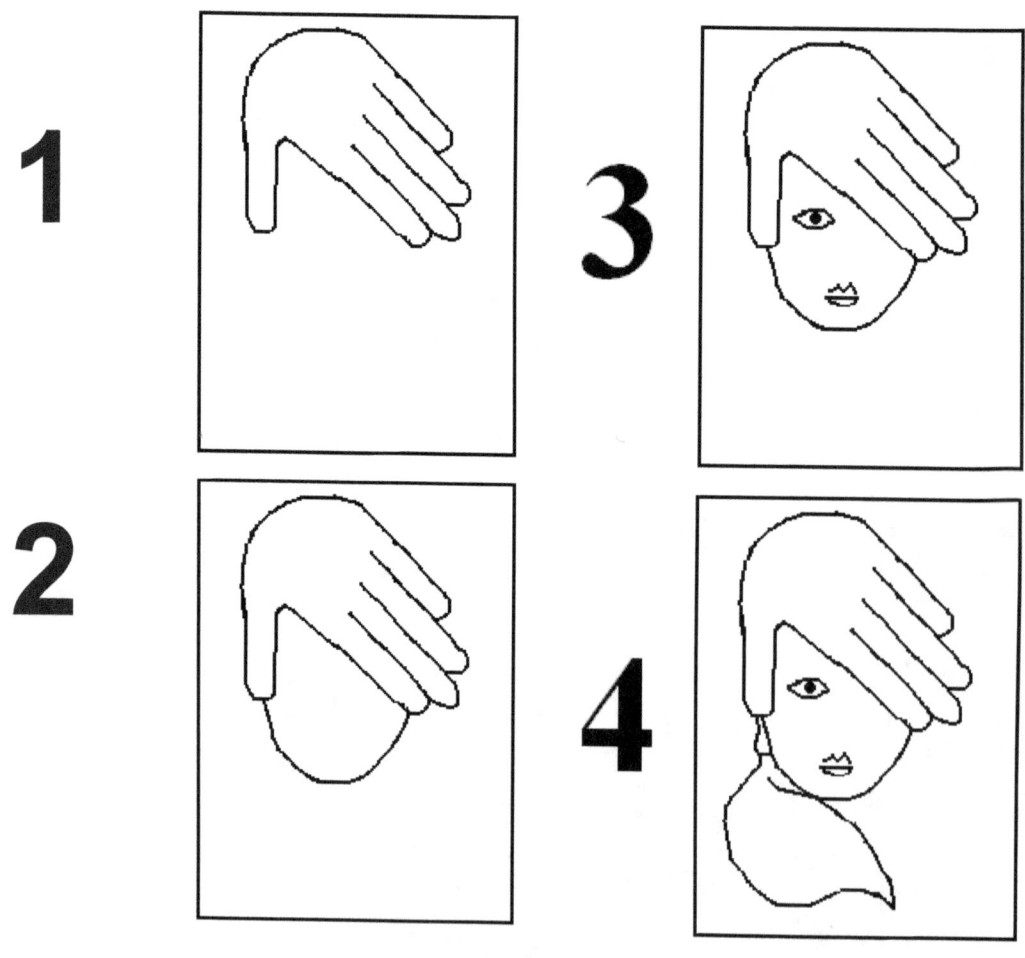

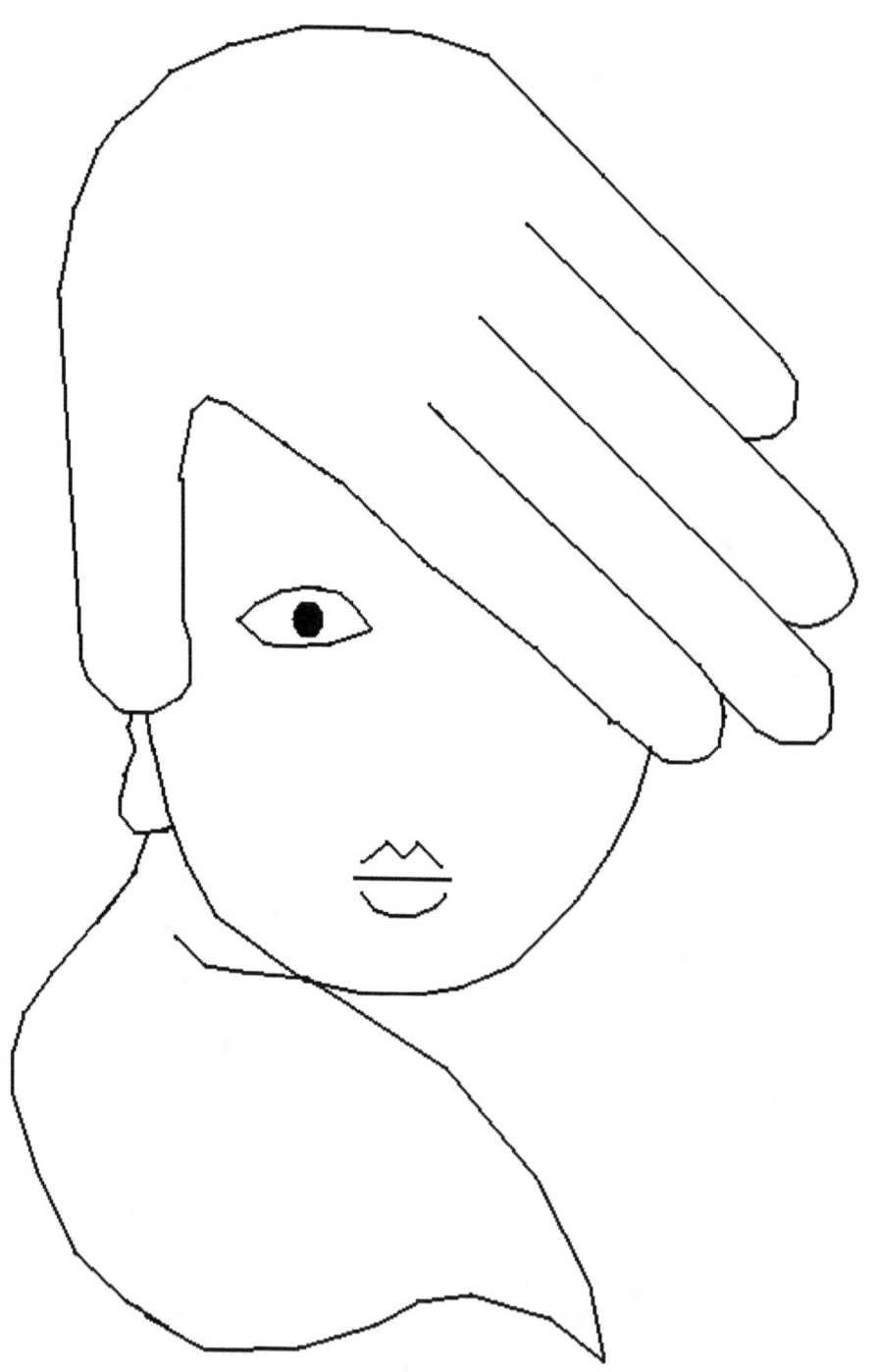

This is the last drawing of the book, but not the last drawing of the method. You can create your own drawings, and in the book "The Hand-Shaped Drawing System vol.2" you can find more great ideas.

# Take Care Of The Environment And Protect Your Planet

*Don't throw garbage on the street.

*Don't burn up trash (even worst if you burn car wheels).

*Don't light up fire on green areas.

*Economize water: close water while soaping when you shower, and while brushing teeth.

*Utilize recycled materials.

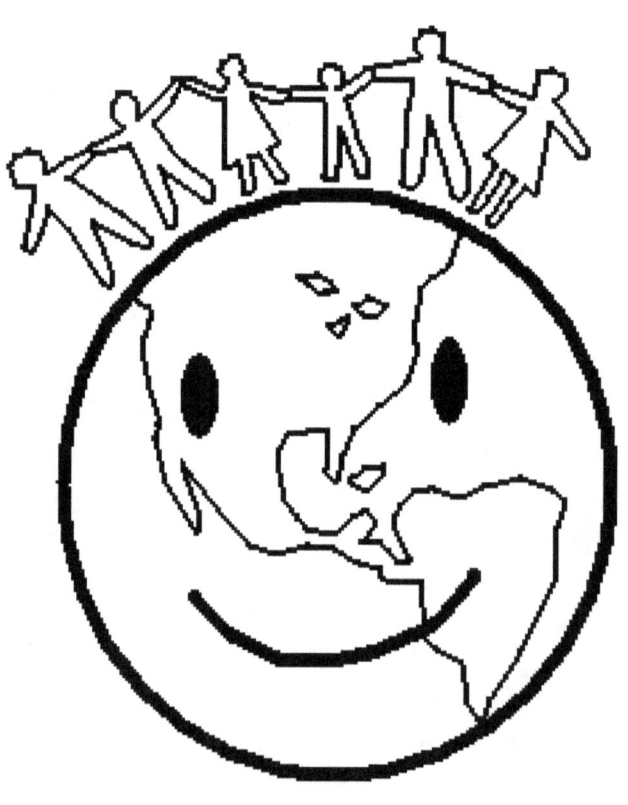

# Index

www.ingramcontent.com/pod-product-compliance
Lightning Source LLC
Chambersburg PA
CBHW081214170526
45165CB00009B/2813